Wolcott's Mining Manual

Containing the U.S. Mining Laws, Arizona and California Mining Laws and Other Things Useful to Miners Everywhere

by N.A. Wolcott

with an introduction by Kerby Jackson

Introduction

It has often been said that "*gold is where you find it*", but even beginning prospectors understand that their chances for finding something of value in the earth or in the streams of the Golden West are dramatically increased by going back to those places where gold and other minerals were once mined by our forerunners. Despite this, much of the contemporary information on local mining history that is currently available is mostly a result of mere local folklore and persistent rumors of major strikes, the details and facts of which, have long been distorted. Long gone are the old timers and with them, the days of first hand knowledge of the mines of the area and how they operated. Also long gone are most of their notes, their assay reports, their mine maps and personal scrapbooks, along with most of the surveys and reports that were performed for them by private and government geologists. Even published books such as this one are often retired to the local landfill or backyard burn pile by the descendents of those old timers and disappear at an alarming rate. Despite the fact that we live in the so-called "Information Age" where information is supposedly only the push of a button on a keyboard away, true insight into mining properties remains illusive and hard to come by, even to those of us who seek out this sort of information as if our lives depend upon it. Without this type of information readily available to the average independent miner, there is little hope that our metal mining industry will ever recover.

This important volume and others like it, are being presented in their entirety again, in the hope that the average prospector will no longer stumble through the overgrown hills and the tailing strewn creeks without being well informed enough to have a chance to succeed at his ventures.

Kerby Jackson
Josephine County, Oregon
May 2018

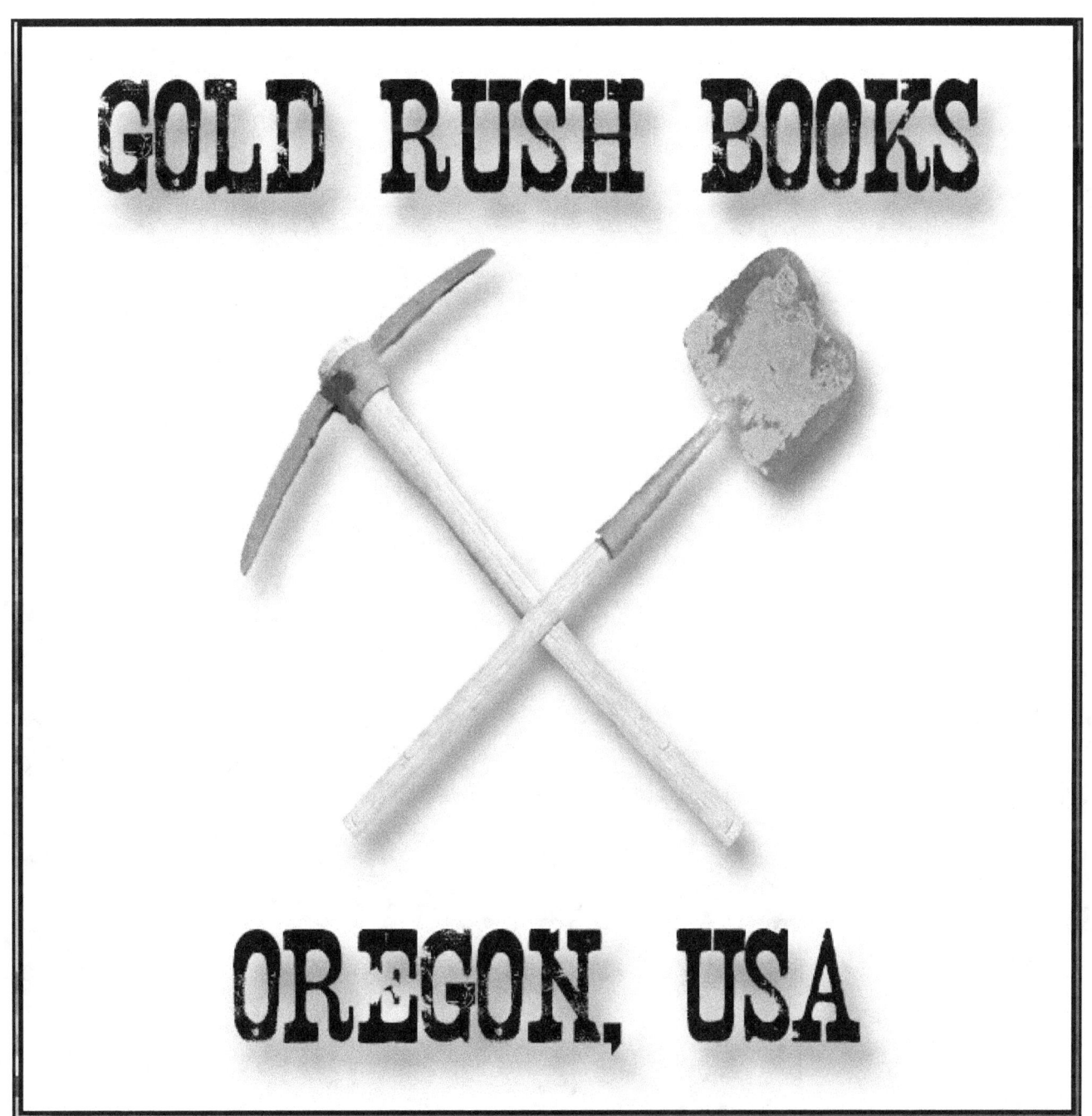

GOLD RUSH BOOKS

OREGON, USA

www.GoldMiningBooks.com

INDEX.

INDEX.

INDEX.

INDEX.

INDEX.

MINING BLANKS

The New Mining Laws of California require that Corporations have filed monthly

A Directors' Report
A Superintendents' Report
A Pay Roll

That Mining Prospectors or Locators shall post, file or record as the case may be

A 1st. Quartz Location Notice
A 2d.   "   "
A 1st. Placer   "
A 2d.   "   "   or affidavit

There are others, Bond for a Deed: The Deed for a Mine, &c. &c.

We print and sell these blanks to all the principal Dealers; if any you ask havn't them, write to us; the price is 30c a doz. $2. per 100

Our blanks are examined by an attorney who makes Mining Law a specialty, and we have no hesitation in saying that all our blanks Legal or Mining Forms, are "Up to date" and the best on the market.

BONDS

Steel Engraved.

These Bonds are very handsome and price for the Bonds completed, printed and numbered is very reasonable.

STOCK CERTIFICATES

We have a Line of designs prepared by a western engraving house which seeks mining patronage; we have others, and all kinds of designs for any business; prices are right.

What About It !

A HANDY, DURABLE BOOK, giving essential information and suitable for the pocket of the prospector,
is what we are aiming to give in this Manual.

We keep the book up to date, as can be perceived
by the dates of the laws given in different parts of
the book.

Hints from men in the field as to what is useful to
them and needed will be useful to us in preparing
future editions.

The Miner comes nearer being the creator of
wealth to-day, as he has for the ages past, than any
other worker on, or in the earth; Of all the sacrifices
that man can make, he makes the most—No height
too dizzy; no depth so deep; no danger so great,
but what he dare go—True, 'tis self interest he seeks,
but who does not? Who spends money like the
miner? Whence comes the golden millions that
grease the wheels of commerce? The miner spends
them; to him we dedicate this book; may it prove
useful to him—help him make his million.

California.

ANNUAL LABOR.—A proof of annual labor and improvements must be filed with the county recorder of the county where the claim is situated not later than the 30th of January succeeding the year in which the work has been performed. Except the year in which the claim is located $100 of Labor or improvements is necessary on each claim every year until a United States patent is obtained.

SALES.—By a new provision passed in 1897, it shall not be lawful for the directors of any mining corporation to sell, lease, mortgage, or otherwise dispose of the whole or any part of the mining ground owned or held by such corporation, nor to purchase or obtain in any way (except by location) any additional mining ground, unless such act be ratified by the holders of at least two-thirds of the stock of such corporation then outstanding. Such ratification may be made either in writing, signed and acknowledged by such stockholders, or by resolution, duly passed at any regularly called stockholders' meeting.

MINING CUSTOMS.—In actions respecting mining claims, proof must be admitted of the customs, usages or regulations established and in force at the bar or diggings embracing such claim; and such customs, usages or regulations, when not in conflict with the laws of this state, must govern the decision of the action.

WATER RIGHTS.—The right to use running water flowing in a river or stream, or down a canyon or a ravine, may be acquired by appropriation. This must be for some useful or beneficial purpose, and when the appropriator or his successor in interest ceases to use it for such a purpose, the right ceases. The person entitled to the use may change the place of diversion, if others are not injured by such change, and may extend the ditch, flume, pipe or aqueduct by which the diversion is made to place beyond the first use. The water appropriated may be turned into the channel of another stream and mingled with its waters, and then reclaimed; but in reclaiming it the water already appropriated by another must not be eliminated. As between appropriators, the one first in time is the first in right. A person desiring to appropriate must post a notice in writing, in a conspicuous place at the point of intended diversion, stating therein: First, that he claims the water there flowing to the extent of (giving the number) inches, measured under a four-inch pressure; second, the purposes for which he claims it, and place of intended use; third, the means by which he intends to divert it and the size of the flume, ditch, pipe or aqueduct in which he intends to divert it. A copy of the notice, within ten days after it is posted, must be recorded in the recorder's office of the county in which it is posted. Within sixty days after the notice is posted the claimant must commence the excavation or construction of the works in which he intends to divert the water, and must prosecute the work diligently and uninterruptedly until completion, unless temporarily interrupted by snow or rain. Completion, means conducting the water to the place of intended use. By a compliance with the above the claimant's right to the use of the water relates back to the time the notice was posted, but a failure deprives the claimant of the right as against a subsequent claimant who complies.

No LOCATION LAW—The People of the State of California represented in Senate and Assembly, do enact as follows:

SECTION 1. An act to repeal "An Act Prescribing the Manner of Locating Mining Claims upon the Public Domain of the United States Recording Notices of Location thereof, Amending Defective Locations and Providing for the Deposit of District Records with County Recorders, and Prescribing the Effect to be Given to Recordation of Notices of Location and Affidavits," approved March 27, 1897, is hereby repealed.

SEC. 2. This act shall take effect immediately. [March 28, 1899]

The California law for location of mining claims having been repealed March 28, 1899, the Federal statute, number 2324, will alone govern in making notice of location of claims in this state.

THE LAW
PROTECTING STOCKHOLDERS.

CHAPTER XLI.

An Act to amend Section 1 and 3 of an Act entitled "An Act for the better protection of the Stockholders in Corporations formed under the laws of the State of California, for the Purpose of Carrying on and Conducting the Business of Mining." approved March 30, 1874.

[Approved February 26, 1897.]

The People of the State of California, represented in the Senate and Assembly, do enact as follows:

SECTION 1. Section one of an Act for the better protection of stockholders in corporations formed under the laws of the State of California for the purpose of carrying on and conducting the business of mining, approved March thirtieth, eighteen hundred and seventy four, is hereby amended so as to read as follows:

SEC. 1. It shall be the duty of the secretary of every corporation formed for the purpose of mining, or conducting mining in California, to keep a complete set of books showing all receipts and expenditures of such corporation, the sources of such receipts, and the objects of such expenditures, and also all transfers of stock. All books and papers shall, at all times during business hours, be open to the inspection of any bona fide stockholder; and if any stockholder shall at any time so request, it shall be the duty of the secretary to attend at the office of said

5

company at least one hour in the day out of regular business hours, and exhibit such books and papers of the company as such stockholders may desire, who shall be entitled to be accompanied by an expert; and he shall also be entitled to make copies or extracts from any such books or papers. Any stockholder may, at reasonable hours, have permission to examine such mining property, and he shall be entitled to be accompanied by an expert to examine such property, to take samples, and to make such other examinations as he may deem necessary. It shall be the duty of the directors on the second Monday of each and every month, to cause to be made an itemized account or balance sheet for the previous month, embracing a full and complete statement of all disbursements and receipts, showing from what sources such receipts were derived, and for what and to whom such disbursements or payments were made, and for what object or purpose the same were made, also all indebtedness or liabilities incurred or existing at the time, and for what the same were incurred, and the balance of money if any, on hand. Such account or balance sheet shall be verified under oath by the president and secretary, and posted in some conspicuous place in the office of the company. It shall be the duty of the superintendent, on the first Monday of each month, to file with the secretary an itemized account, verified under oath, showing all receipts and disbursements made by him for the previous month and for what said disbursements were made. Such accounts shall, also, contain a verified statement showing the number of men employed under him, and for what purpose, and the rate of wages paid to each one. He shall attach to such account a full and complete report, under oath, of the work done in said mine, the amount of ore extracted, from what part of the mine taken, the amount sent to mill for reduction, its assay value, the amount of bullion received, the amount of bullion shipped to the office of the company or elsewhere, and the amount, if any, retained by the superintendent. It shall also be his duty to forward to the office of the company a full report, under oath, of all discoveries of ores or mineral-bearing quartz made in said mine whether by boring, drifting, sinking or otherwise, together with the assay value thereof. All accounts, reports, and correspondence from the superintendent shall be kept in some conspicuous place in the office of said company, and to be open to the inspection of all stockholders.

PROVIDED, That this section shall apply only to mining corporations whose stock is listed and offered for sale at public exchange, and shall not apply to mining corporations whose stock is not listed in the public exchange and is not offered for public sale

SEC. 2. Section three of said Act is hereby amended so as to read as follows:

SEC. 3. In case of the refusal or neglect of the president to cause to be issued by the secretary the order in the second section of this Act mentioned, such stockholder shall be entitled to recover against said president the sum of one thousand dollars and costs as provided in the last section. In case of the failure of the directors to have the reports and accounts current made and posted as in the first section of this Act provided, they shall be liable, either severally or jointly, to an action by any stockholder in any court of competent jurisdiction complaining thereof and on proof of such refusal or failure, such complaining stockholder shall recover judgment for actual damages sustained by him, with costs of suit. And each of such defaulting directors shall also be liable to removal for such neglect.

This Act shall take effect immediately.

Section two of the original enactment is as follows

CHAPTER DCXXVII.

Of the laws of the State of California for Years 1873-1874.

SEC. 2. Any owner of stock of the par value of five hundred dollars in any of the corporations mentioned in section one of this Act, shall at all hours of business or labor on or about the premises or property of such Corporation, have the right to enter upon such property and examine the same, either on the surface or under ground, and it is hereby made the duty of any and all officers, managers, agents, superintendents or persons in charge, to allow any such stockholder to enter upon and examine any of the property of such Corporation at any time during the hours of business or labor; and the presentation of certificates of stock in the Corporation of the par value of five hundred dollars, to the officer or the person in charge, shall be prima facie evidence of ownership and right to enter upon or into, and make examinations of the property of the Corporation.

Gilsonite.

This is a name given to the purest form of Asphaltum found in the United States, or in the world, and has been applied to that material especially found in Utah. It is used for many purposes, but especially for paints, varnishes and insulation for wire. The name is given it in honor of Mr. Gilson the discoverer.

Hardness of Minerals.

This is expressed in the following scale of ten degrees:

1.	Diamond,	10	4.	Quartz,	7	7.	Fluorspar,	4
2.	Corundum,	9	5.	Feldspar,	6	8.	Calcite,	3
3.	Topaz,	8	6.	Apatile,	5	9.	Gypsum,	2
						10.	Talc.	1

Gold.

Gold is known as the King of metals, and is the standard of values throughout the civilized world.

It is never found pure in its native state. The purest native gold known is from Mount Morgan, Queensland, Australia, said to contain 98.7 to 99.8 per cent of gold, a little copper and iron, and a trace of silver.

Silver is always present in all native gold and its amount may be judged from the color of the metal unless this is masked by other causes.

The average richness of Australian gold is from 92 to 92.5 per cent. Of California gold 88 per cent, although it varys largely in this State according to the location in which it is found. For instance, the gold from the neighborhood of El Toro and Capistrano in the Southern part of this State is worth only about $13.50 per ounce: gold from San Gabriel canyon, Goler and Red Rock is usually valued in payment for goods at $17.40 per ounce, although that from Red Rock is worth at least 50 cents per ounce more than that from the other two localities. Gold from near Saugus and Newhall is valued at $18.50 per ounce just as it is taken from the ground.

Pure gold has an orange yellow color, a bright lustre when polished and is not oxidized or tarnished by the air, but becomes darkened, or nearly black when in contact with sulphur.

Pure gold is valued at $20-67 per ounce by the mints throughout the world. A pennyweight of gold is generally figured at $1.03 per pennyweight, but its actual value is $1.0335.

The gold coin in the United States consists of .9 pure gold and .1 alloy, and is not quite 22 carat fine.

A new law has recently been passed by which it is a criminal offence to purposely mutilate United States coins, or to pass such coins.

The specific gravity of pure gold is 19.25: its symbol is Au., being an abbreviation of the chemical and latin name for gold which is Aurum. Its equivalent is 197, that is when it combines chemically with other elements, or combinations of elements, there is always exactly 197 parts of gold in the combination.

Gold is not attacked or dissolved by any simple acid, but can be dissolved by a combination of nitric and hydrochloric acids, called Aqua Regia, meaning King of Waters, for the reason that it dissolves the king of metals.

Absolutely pure gold is the same color the world over, unless discolored chemically

Gold is found in its native state mixed with sands of the rivers and oceans, and when in this form is saved by washing with water, either in pans, rockers or sluices. Mercury is often used in this process to facilitate the saving of the gold.

Gold is also found in combination with other metals, and also sometimes in the free state in quartz and other rocks. In fact it has been demonstrated of late years that gold is where you find it, for the reason that it has been found in minerals which it was supposed a few years ago could never carry gold.

Gold found in ores, or rocks, is often in combination with sulphur and other metal when it is called sulphurets. It is has been a grave mistake in California in past years for miners to pass over sulphurets in their search for free gold, but it is now a fact that many mines are being worked to a profit where the gold is entirely in the form of sulphurets. In fact a good sulphuret proposition is considered of almost as much value as a free gold ore of about the same value per ton. The Cyanide process has recently made rapid strides in the saving of gold contained in sulphurets.

Silver.

Silver is a white metal which will take by polishing a bright lustre. Its symbol is Ag., its equivalent 108.1 and its specific gravity 10.5. It is found in a pure state in nature, very often in combination with metallic copper, but most often in combination with sulphur, known as sulphurets. It is also found occasionally in combination with chlorine, when it is usually called horn silver. Owing to the demonitizing of silver by the leading nations of the world, its value has fallen from $1.29 per ounce to 60 cents per ounce at the present time. This immense decrease in value has had the effect of closing a large number of silver mines which cannot be worked at a profit at the present low price of silver.

Silver is found in more or less quantities throughout the Pacific Coast and other western states and territories.

Copper.

At the present time, owing to the rapid strides in the science of electricity, and the various uses to which copper can be put for electrical purposes, this metal has been gradually increasing in value for the past two years.

The present price of copper in New York, in large lots is about 11 1-2 cents per pound.

Its specific gravity is 8.78, its symbol Cu., and the equivalent 31.7.

Copper is found in the metallic state in large masses in Michigan, and in smaller quantities in other parts of the United States. The form from which most of the copper in this country is obtained, is in combination with sulphur, known as copper pyraties. Although considerable copper is obtained from ores containing carbonates of copper.

Lead.

Lead has a very extensive commercial use and is mostly obtained from galena, or sulphuret of lead.

This ore usually carries gold, and especially silver, sometimes in quite large quantities.

It is a general rule among mining men that where galena contains large well defined crystals, it carries much less quantities of gold and silver than when the formation is a very small crystal or almost granular. Although this is not an invariable rule.

Owing to the large production of this metal of late years, cheaper processes for working it, and the reduction of import duties, lead has been gradually falling in value until now it is worth about $3.12 per 100 pounds. It is expected, however; that it will rise in value with the inauguration of a new tariff.

Troy Weights.

All precious metals are weighed by Troy weights, which are as follows: 24 grains=1 pwts. 20 pwts.=1 oz., 12 ozs. 1=lb.

To reduce Av. to Troy weights: 1 lb. Av.=7,000 Troy grains. Weigh your bullion in pounds and ounces Av. and reduce it to grains. Divide the number of grains thus obtained by 480, the number of grains to a troy ounce: this will give you the number of Troy ounces. If any grains are left divide them by 24, number of grains to a pennyweight. This will give you the number of pennyweights; any grains left after the last division are Troy grains, giving you the result in ounces, pennyweights and grains Troy.

Troy grains, ounces and pounds are exactly the same as Apothecaries weights. There are 5,760 grains to a pound Troy and a pound Apothecary weight.

14 1-2 Ounces Troy equals a pound Av.

As an illustration for reducing Av. weights into Troy, say we have 3 pounds 7 1-2 ozs. Av. weight of bullion. Multiply 7,000 grains by 3, which equals 21,000 grains. As there are 16 ounces to a pound Av. the 7 1-2 ounces would equal 7 1-2 16ths or 15 32nds of 7,000, which equals 3281 1-4 Troy grains. added to the 21,000 equals 24,281 1-4 grains, divide this by 480, the number of grains to a Troy ounce and you have 50 ounces. 281 1-4 grains: divide

281 ¼ by 24, the number of grains to a pennyweight and you have 11 pennyweights, 17 ¼ grains. Result: 3 lbs. 7 ½ ounces Av. equals 50 ounces, 11 pwts. 17 ¼ grains Troy.

Diamonds are weighed by carats, four Troy grains equaling 1 carat.

A miners inch of water is the quantity which will pass through a square inch hole under a four inch pressure in one minute, and equals 1.15 cubic feet, or 8.97 gallons of water per minute.

Specific Gravity.

The Specific gravity of a metal or mineral means that a cubic inch or a cubic foot of the metal or mineral is as many times heavier than a cubic inch or a cubic foot of rain water than the specific gravity marked against the metal.

As an illustration, the specific gravity of pure gold is 19.25, therefore it is 19 and one fourth times the weight of rain water.

A cubic foot of water weighs 62 ½ pounds, therefore a cubic foot of gold would weigh 19 ¼ times that, which equals 1203.1 pounds.

The specific gravity of quartz is from 2.5 to 2.8, according to the impurities it may contain, such as gold, sulphurets, oxide of iron, etc.

It is generally estimated that 13 cubic feet of solid quartz in place equals 1 ton, and that quartz when broken increases in bulk three-fourths of its measure, consequently it would take 22 ¾ cubic feet of broken quartz to weigh a ton of 2,000 lbs.

The above figures are not absolutely correct, as the specific gravity of quartz from the different mines is not always the same, but the figures are close enough for ordinary purposes.

Solid Measure.

1,728 cubic inches equals 1 cubic foot.
27 cubic feet equals 1 cubic yard.

London and New York Silver Quotations.

The highest New York Silver quotations in 1890, after the Sherman act was passed, was 119¾, when it took a steady decline and never recovered.

The bank of England suspended specie payment Feburary 27, 1797, and resumed payment May 1st, 1823, having made four years preparation.

The London price is given in pence per ounces of silver 925-1000 fine. New York price is given in cents at 1000 fine. The pound sterling is $4.8665, for calculation in the U. S. Treasury Department. Having London prices given in pence for silver, multiply that by .02192, and you will have its equivalent in cents for fine silver.

Sure Thing !--Gold is Where You Find It.

"Surely there is a vein for silver and a place for Gold where they find it."—Job 1-28.

Bulk of the World's Coin Supply.

If all the silver in the world coined as money were melted into a solid cube it could be contained in a room 66 feet square and 66 feet high with room to spare. If all the gold coin in the world were similarly treated, a room 22 feet square and 22 feet high would hold it without being wholly filled. The best authorities estimate the total sum of silver money in the world at 3,750 million of dollars, and the total value of gold money of the world at 3,800 millions of dollars.

What Gives Gold its Commercial Value.

The Bank of England (under the act of July 19, 1844, Sec. 4) issues its notes in payment for all gold offered at the rate of

£3,17s, 10½d per ounce.(Standard or 11-12 fine, or 440 fine grains), equal to $20.671, for one ounce of fine gold of 480 grains. The United States mints also issue gold coin for all gold deposited, at the same rate.

THE UNIT VALUE OF LEAD ORE, based on New York quotations at $4.00 per 100 lbs:

Each per cent of lead contained in ore is equal to as many units. Ore carrying 50 per cent of lead (or 50 units) is worth for example, 60 cents per unit, or 50 times 60, equals $30 per ton if New York quotations is $4.00 per hundred. For each decline or rise of 5 cent in the New York price a deduction or addition of one cent should be made. For instance: If the New York quotation on the day of settlement is $3.95, then 1 cent from the price (60 cents) should be taken, making 59 cents as the settlement price, and so on down to the present quotation of $3.15 (Sept. 26, 1895,) when 17 cents from 60 leaves 43 cents per unit. Therefore ore carrying 50 per cent lead would amount to 50x43=$21.50 per ton.

This method has been generally adopted throughout this State for the settlement of lead ores.

Value of Metals.

	Lb. Avoirdupois.
Aluminum, bar,	$ .50
Antimony,	.10
Bismuth, crude,	1.95
Copper,	.11
Gold,	299.72
Lead,	.03¼
Mercury,	.32½
Platinum,	182.00
Silver Bullion,	8.70
Tin,	.19

Zinc,	-	-	-	-	-	.04
Arsenic,	-	-	-	-	-	.10
Nickel,	-	-	-	-	-	.45
Vanadium, Crystal, fused,		-	-	-		4800.00

Weight of Ore.

One cube foot of water, 62.4 lbs.

			Wt. of Cubic Foot.	Cu. Ft. in one Ton.
Quartz,	-	Lbs.	162	12.34
Silver Glance,	-	"	455	4.39
Ruby Silver,	-	"	362	5.52
Light Ruby Silver,		"	336	5.95
Stephanite, B. S.,	-	"	386	5.18
Horn Silver,	-	"	345	5.80
Stibnite, Antimony Glance,			287	6.99
Cinnabar,	-	"	549	3.64
Copper Pyrities,	-	"	262	7.63
Grey Copper,	-	"	280	7.14
Galena,	-	"	461	4.34
Sphalerite [Blende]		"	249	8.03
Iron Pyrities,	-	"	312	6.41
Limestone,	-	"	174	11-50
Clay,	-	"	162	12.34

Gold Values.

1 oz. Troy pure gold is worth	-		-	$	20.67.
1 pennyweight [dwt]	-	-	-		1.03
1 grain,	-	-	-	-	0.04⅓
1 oz. avoirdupois,	-	-	-		18.84
1 lb. "	-	-	-		301.37
1 ton [2000 lbs.]	-	-	-		602,737,.20

MINING DICTIONARY.

Acequia—A ditch.

Adit—A horizontal drift or passage opening to or draining a mine, applied to no level except one opening on the surface.

Adventurer—A shareholder.

Alligator—A rock breaker operating by jaws.

Alluvium—The sediment of streams and floods.

Amalgam—The mechanical combination of quicksilver with gold or silver.

Apex—The top of a mineral vein.

Arastra—A circular mill for grinding quartz by trituration between stones attached loosely to cross arms.

Arch—A part of the gangue left standing for support.

Argentiferous—Silver bearing.

Ascension Theory—Referring to the filling of fissures with matter from below.

Assay—An assayed test for mineral contained in a larger mass by extracting and weighing a portion.

Assessment Work—The $100 labor required to hold a claim.

Attle—Waste rock.

Auriferous—Gold bearing.

Back—The roof of a drift, stope or other working.

Bal—A mine.

Bank—The surface at the pit's mouth.

Banksman—The man at the mouth of the shaft who handles the bucket.

Bar Diggings—Gold washed on river-bars

Barriers—Posts of unworked gangue or coal left to prevent drainage from mine to mine.

Base Bullion—Pig lead containing its gold and silver unseparated.

Base Metals—All metals except gold, silver, mercury and platinum groups which are termed Noble Metals.

Bed—A horizontal seam or deposit of ore.

Bed Rock—The solid rock underlying the gravel, slide or other loose earth.

Bismuth—An alloy chiefly; at. wt. 210, Symbol Bi., hard, brittle, grayish color.

Black Jack—A dark variety of Zinc blende.

Blende—A sulphide of Zinc.

Blossom—Decomposed out-crop of a vein; Gossan; Iron hat.

Blow-out—A spreading out-crop.

Bonanza—A large body of paying ore; a familiar term applied to the Comstock.

Booming—Placer mining where water is accumulated in dams and used in torrents.

Boom Ditch—A ditch from the dam in booming; also a narrow ditch down a declivity into which sudden heads of water are turned intending to cut bed rock or prospect for the apex of underlying lodes.

Borraska—Played out mine.

Boulder—Large round loose stone or pebble.

Breast—The heading of a drift, tunnel or other horizontal working.

Breccia—Conglomerate of angular fragments.

Brittle Silver—Stephanite; Sulphide of Antimony and Silver; 68½ per cent Silver with the Antimony variable; sometimes contains iron, copper and arsenic; variable in color, hardness and specific gravity.

Broaching—Straightening up and trimming.

Buddling—Separating ores by washing.

Bullion—Gold or silver uncoined; Base Bullion; Pig Lead with gold and silver

Cache—A prospectors hiding place for outfit or provision.

Calamine—Ore of zinc.

Cage—The frame of the car.

Canyon—Precipitous mountain valley.

Cap—The space where the walls contract leaving only a trace of the vein.

Carbonates—An ore of lead and silver; a salt formed by union of carbolic acid with a base; lead as a base makes soft carbonate; Iron for a base, makes hard carbonate.

Cement—Gold bearing gravel hardened into a mass.

Chaffee Work—Referring to annual labor; Jerome B. Chaffee was delegate from Colorado, and was instrumental in passing the mining act of 1872.

Cheek—Wall or side of a vein.

Chimney—An ore body or pocket with a perpendicular direction.

Chlorides—Combination of chlorine with other elements.

Chute (or shoot)—A trough or flume for sliding ore; a chimney of ore.

Cinnabar—Sulphite of mercury.

Claim—A location of land for mining purposes; The right to mine upon a location.

Clean-up—Collecting the gold which has settled in the flumes or in the arastras.

18

Cleavage—Splitting; lamination; fracturing more easily in certain directions.

Coaster—A miner who picks over the dumps of abandoned mines for the ore in sight.

Cobalt—A tough, reddish gray mineral.

Cobbing—Ore sorting.

Coin—To make metal into money by stamping it metal currency.

Collar—The top of a shaft or winze and when carried above the surface.

Color—Particles of gold in the pan.

Concentration—Removal of ore from the gangue or slime.

Contact—The plane on which two formations meet.

Contact Vein—The vein along the plane of Contact of two dissimilar formations; hence separating them.

Copper—Metal; Reddish; Ductile; Malleable; Tenacious; Fuses 1996 deg. Fahr., Symbol Cu. Atomic Weight 63½ Spec. grav. 8.9

Cost-Book Company—The mining partnerships common to Cornwall and Devon, England.

Country Rock—The strata outside the mineral vein or lode.

Course of Vein—Its strike; the horizontal line on which it intersects Country rock.

Coyoting---Irregular surface mining.

Cradle—A short trough or rocker for washing gold.

Cribbing—Timber frame work, rough or light for lining shafts, drifts, winze or mill holes.

Creosote—The creosote of commerce (not true Creosote) for timber preservation, contains 8 per cent tar acids or phenols; Carbolic and Cresylic Acids; about 20 per cent Napthalene; about 30 per cent heavy residuum after distillation up to 600 deg. Fahr. consisting of anthracene and pitch; the remainder light and heavy oils, no water nor ammonia and must be the product of bituminous coal tar only; this excludes wood tar and petroleum tar.

Cross Course—An intersecting vein.

Cross Cut—A level driven across the course of a vein; A short tunnel.

Cut—To intersect a vein; open cut; a horizontal opening at the surface not reaching over.

Cyanide—A compound of Cyanogen with a metal; The cyanide process is the passing of the gold solution of cyanide potassium over zinc shavings thereby causing precipitation.

Dead Riches—Base Bullion.

Dead Work—Sinking shafts; Running drifts; Adits or cross cuts; it may embrace any work which is non-productive of ore, except stoping and its timbering.

Debris—Loose waste rock of any kind.

Deep—The lower part of a Vein.

Denouncement—Spanish and Mexican term for "location and record" of a claim.

Descension Theory—That theory that the veins were filled from the top.

Diggings—Placer mines.

Dike—A fissure caused and filled by plutonic action; It is usually barren but often times carries a mineralized selvage and appears as the wall of the lode.

Diluvium—Deposits of loose boulders earth etc., and attributed geologically to water action.

Dip—The departure of a vein from a straight line.

Ditch—An artificial water way, flume or canal.

Divining Rod—A witch hazel stick or similar device used for prospecting.

Dollar—(German Thaler) U. S. 100 cents Gold 23.22 grains fine; Silver 371¼ grains fine; Mexican 377.17 grains fine.

Drift—A tunnel driven horizontally on or with the ore vein.

Downcast—Ventilating shaft with descending draft.

Dump—The place of deposit or the deposit of refuse or waste rock and tailings.

Elvan Course—A plutonic dike.

Exploitation—Active work succeeding the prospecting stage.

Eye—The top of shaft.

Face—The breast; the heading of a drift or tunnel.

Fathom—6 feet forward and 6 feet vertical with the width of the vein.

Fault—The dislocation of a vein from its original position; A throw; A heave.

Feeder—A spur; A small vein running into the main lode.

Feldspar—A crystalline constituent of granite, gneiss, porphyry, etc.

Fissure—A cleft or crack; A longitudinal opening.

Fissure Vein—A fissure or crack across the strata containing mineral body.

Float—Loose quartz found near or below the vein.

Float ore—Detached particles or masses of ore below the vein.

Flookan—A decomposed soft cross course.

Floor—The rock underlying a horizontal vein.

Flume—A wooden box like ditch built in frames.

Foot Wall—The under wall of the vein.

Forfeiture—The loss of title because of abandonment or failure to perform the conditions requisite.

20

Gad---Small pointed wedge.

Galena---Lead Sulphite; The principal ore of Lead; amorphous, or is crystallized in cubes; when pure, has 86.6 per cent lead, 13.4 per cent sulphur, carries silver.

Gallery---A level or drift usually referring to coal mining.

Gangue---Crevice material; The base material forming the matrix of the ore.

Gash Vein---Short vein below the sod narrowing as it descends.

Geode---The cavity in an irregular rounded stone or nodule, studded with Crystals or mineral.

Gneiss---Crystalline rock foliated or stratified.

Gob Fire---Colliery fire produced by spontaneous combustion.

Gold---Metal Yellow, spec. grav. 19.34 fuses 2016 deg. Fahr. Symbol Au. atomic weight 196.6; one ounce of pure gold is worth intrinsically and commercially, as established by the Bank of England's Notes issued for gold, $20.67 U. S. Gold Coin.

Gossan---Iron hat; The out-crop of a lode.

Gouge---A soft selvage; A clay streak found following a wall; A slip or an ore measure.

Grass--- The Surface over a mine.

Grass Roots---A term used where a working is started from the surface.

Granite---Rock consisting of quartz, feldspar and mica.

Gray Copper---Tetrahedrite; ore containing 15 to 42 per cent copper, with iron, zinc, silver, mercury, arsenic and antimony.

Grub Stake---Staking a prospector with provision and necessities on a contract to share the proceeds of his discoveries.

Gut---To rob a mine; To work for ore in sight only, regardless of any damage to supports, etc.

Hanging Wall---Upper wall of the vein.

Heading---The face of a working.

Headings---Pay dirt and gravel above the head of a sluice.

Heave---Horizontal dislocation of a lode by another.

High Explosives---Explosives of greater detonating power than powder.

Hitches---Abrupt turnings in a drift.

Horse---Country Rock between the walls of a vein which converges about the mass below and at both ends but not overhead.

Hudge---Iron bucket for hoisting.

Hydraulics---Placer mining with water under pressure.

Hungry---Barren rock.

Impregnation---Metallic deposit having no sharply defined limits.

Incline Drift---An inclined drift to aid drainage; also a misnomer applied to a slope sunk upon a deposit having a slight departure from the horizontal.

Infiltration Theory---The theory which refers to the origin of the ore bodies to the depositing of minerals from the water which held them in solution.

Injection Theory---That theory which ascribes the origin of ores to the introduction of igneous fluid.

In Place---Rock in place as contra distinguished from soil or debris. It is in place though broken and loose, when within well defined walls.

Iron Hat---Gossan; the out-crop of a lode: it is usually shown by decomposition of the iron.

Jig---A machine of sieves for concentrating ores.

Jump---To take illegal possession of a claim by force or to relocate an abandoned claim.

Kibble---A hoisting bucket.

Lagging---Small timber or poles used for Spanning from one stull-piece to another, for cribbing mill-holes and for lining behind the timbers of a shaft.

Lead---Ledge or lode.

Lead---A soft heavy metal bluish white, fuses at 617 deg. Fahr., Symbol Pb. atomic weight 207; Spec. grav. 11.30 Galena and carbonates are its most common ore.

Ledge---Lode or lead; an aggregation of mineral matter in ores distributed in veins in the earth.

Length---A portion of the vein when taken in a horizontal line.

Level---A drift along the vein where there are a series of drifts, as one hundred ft. level; five hundred ft. level, etc.

Lift---Space between two levels.

Little Giant---A nozzle and jointed iron pipe with decreasing diameter and consequent increasing hydraulic power for placer mines.

Location---The several successive acts whereby a mining property is acquired, also the claim itself.

Lode---A ledge or lead a metallic ore body traversing the earth in a continous course or vein.

22

Man Hole---The opening for access between two workings.

Matrix (To the lode)---The country rock in which the vein is found (To the ores) the vein stone, the rock or earthy material enclosing the ore.

Mercury---Quicksilver; a metal; shining silvery white; liquid above 40 deg. Fahr., spec. grav. 13.5; at. wt 199.7; boils at 669 deg, Fahr., Symbol Hg.

Metallurgy---Working of metals including smelting, refining, and the art of parting minerals from their native ores.

Mica---Non-metal; a constituent of granite when separately crystallized it cleaves into clear elastic plates of extreme thinness It is found in the lode and also in the matrix.

Mill Hole---The passage left in the stope for throwing down rock and ore.

Mill Run---The mill returns on a lot of ore as distinguished from a sample assay.

Mine---An excavation usually subterranean for digging minerals also a developed lode as distinguished from a prospect.

Miners Inch---1½ cubic feet of water per minute flowing through a square inch opening in a flume with a 1½ inch fall for every 12 feet, for Colorado; for California, it is the flow of .02 part of a cubic foot per second.

Miners Right---The license to locate, as required in Canada and British possessions.

Moyle---Drill or short bar with a sharp point for cutting hitches and in broaching.

Money---A currency used for simplifying the exchange of the things of commerce, having certain ascribed but fictitious values stated on each piece, such value being fixed by government enactment; whether the article of currency be a metal piece a commodity, or a piece of paper, it is money if it have a stated value stamped upon it and it is passed from person to person in payment for credits or things; Bank checks are rapidly attaining current use to such an extent as to be called secondary money. The value of Gold money is established by the Bank of England's Bank Notes (act July 19, 1844.. Sec. 4.) which are issued in payment for gold per oz. at the rate of £ 3, 17 s-,10½d.

Nodule---A rounded and irregular shaped stone with a marked concavity.

Open Cut---An outside longitudinal working.

Operator---The one who operates or works the mine whether he be owner or lessee.

Ore---The mechanical or chemical compounds of mineral with baser substances. Dry ore;An ore containing none or not over 5 per cent lead. Milling Ore;A dry ore that can be amalgamated or treated by leaching and other process usually low grade and nearly free from base metals. Shipping Ore;Any ore of greater value than freight and cost of treatment. Refactory Ore;An ore that cannot be economically treated by usual process, such as contain quanities of zinc, arsenic, antimony or other bace metals.

Ore Reserves---The exposed ore body ready for stoping.

Out-crop---The end of a vein appearing at the surface.

Out-put---The gross product of the mine.

Pan--- A shallow iron basin for prospecting gold.

Patch---Small placer outside of the main gulch.

Patio--The place where ore is amalgamated by the treading of horses, also a yard or court.

Patio Process---The Mexican way of amalgamation of silver ores.

Pay---Referring to the ore containing the mineral whether they are profitable to work or not.

Pay Rock---The lode matter in which the mineral or pay is found.

Pay Streak---The ore vein or the decomposed material which takes its place and preserves its continuity.

Pent House--.A barricade across one end of a shaft made of strong timbers loaded with rock for protection from accidental fall from above.

Phonolite---A greyish, compact feldspatic rock; gives a metallic sound under the hammer; clinkstone.

Pinch---The space where the walls come close together.

Pit---A hole in the ground; shallow shaft.

Pitch---The incline angle or dip of the lode.

Placer---Loose gold deposits of all forms not found in quartz or other rock in place or vein; also cement diggings; old channels; drift digging and and gulch claims; kaolin or fire clay; borax beds, soda, sulphur, alum and asphaltum, phosphate, stone for lime, petroleum (U. S. Statutes Febr. 11, 1897) (rock salt excepted,) building stone and glass sand and stone of special commercial value.

Plat---A recess or small chamber on the side of a level where it intersects a shaft to facilitate dumping; if cut in the sole it is called a trip-plat.

24

Pocket—A comparatively small detached body of pay ore.

Pockety—Applied to claims containing small detached pay ore bodies.

Porphyry—A variously colored compact rock showing well formed crystals usually of feldspar on a granular base of the same.

Porphyritic Granite—A granite base containing prominent crystals of feldspar.

Prospecting—The searching for mineral deposits in the sense of exploration, examination, and assaying.

Pyrites—When white, is sulphide of iron; when yellow, is a sulphide of copper. A very common gold bearing ore usually of a low grade, crystallized form, bright and metallic looking—commonly called "Iron."

Quarry—Open workings upon the plan of stone quarries; as distinguished from shafts, tunnels etc.

Quartz—Silica; a crystalline form of silica; a rock crystal; a constituent of granite, also a broad term applied to the ore; the float; the gangue or that part which indicates the pay streak—the U. S. statutes use the word (quartz, or other rock) in the sense of pay rock.

Quartzite—A rock containing about 98 per cent silica and a small percentage of other matter, principally iron.

Quicksilver—Mercury; shining silvery white, liquid above 40 deg. Fahr., sp. gr., 13.5; at. wt., 199.7; boils at 669 deg. Fahr., Symbol Hg. A metal.

Raise—Rise; a winze or shaft which has been worked from below.

Rhyolite—A common name given to igneous rocks of a wavy texture showing evidence of flowing or movement when in a former fluid state.

Riffle Blocks or Bars—The sections of cross timbers set on the bottom of sluices having irregular spaces between, to catch and settle the gold.

Reef—The term used in Australia for our ledge or lode.

Rob—Gutting a mine; working for everything in sight, disregarding any benefits or damages to the physical condition of the property.

Rock Conveyor—A contrivance of block and tackle and cable for carrying rocks.

Rocker—A cradle or short rocker for gold washing.

Roof—The stratum of rock over a flat vein or deposit.

Royalty—The percentage or share due the lessor.

Rust—Oxidized; term applied to gold; will not easily amalgamate; ore coated with oxide.

Salt—Chloride of sodium; a non-metallic mineral; refined it is used for seasoning food; also a chemical combination with a base. A kind of mining swindle by means of false ore etc.

Sandstone—A rock made of sand and more or less firmly united, used largely for building material.

Scale—Loosened rocks threatening to fall.

Schist—Crystalline or metamorphic rock with slaty structure usually carrying mica.

Segregations—Bodies of ore having irregular form but definite limits. They differ from beds and lodes by the irregularity of their form from impregnations by their definite limits.

Selvage—A thin band of clay often found in the vein, upon the wall; a Lining; a Gouge; a Slip.

Set—The piece of ground taken by the Tributer.

Serpentine—A mineral or rock spotted or mottled like a serpent's skin. The colors vary.

Shaft—A perpendicular (or nearly) opening; a hole or pit sunk from the surface in order to reach the vein.

Shale—A fine grained slaty rock.

Shift—A change; the miner's turn about or spell of work, day "shift" and night "shift."

Sill—Frame of a windlass.

Silver—Metal; white; specific grav. 10.53; fuses 1073 deg.; Symbol Ag., at. wt. 108; 1 ounce of 480 grains of pure silver coined into metal currency of the United States of America represents a like gold valuation of $1.2929, but it is never so coined: the U. S. dollar contains of pure silver 371¼ grains; the Mexican dollar contains 377.17 grains pure silver. The Bank of England does not recognize silver as money but quotes it this day at 23¾d, 925 fine: equal to New York price of 51¼c, 1000 fine. This means that an American silver dollar is worth to the Bank of England about 39c and a Mexican silver dollar is worth about 41c. (Sept, 11th, 1897).

Silver Glance—An ore; when pure it contains 87 per cent. silver and 13 per cent. sulphur.

Skip—A square hoisting box or bucket running in grooves or guides.

Slate—A dark stone which readily splits into plates.

Slickensides—The polished or smooth parts of the wall or of some vertical plane in the lode, caused by friction; it may occur on the ore.

Slide—The vertical dislocation of a lode; also the mass of loose rock overlying either the lode or the country.

Slope—An opening upon the inclination of the vein.

Sluice—A series of boxes set in line having riffle blocks in the bottom.

Smelting—The reduction of metals from their ores. In smelting the ore is melted: in other processes it is roasted.

Soda—Non-metallic; An alkali. forming the basis for common salt, sodium oxide, carbonate etc.

Sole—Floor of a horizontal working.

Sollar—Any wooden platform or floor or covering in a working.

Sough—The drain.

Spar---A non-metallic mineral; a common term applied to rock with a distinct cleavage and lustre.

Spelter—Zinc.

Spiling—Timbering used in quicksand and loose earth, where lathes are driven behind timbers and kept flush with the heading.

Spur—An offshoot of the main vein; a lateral projection of a mountain.

Stake--To put up funds or provision and neccessaries for a prospector.

Stamp—To crush ore; the loaded steel shoe held vertically in grooves, where being raised and suddenly loosed, falls and crushes the ore, which is placed underneath. Stamp Mills are referred to as "2 stamps," "5 stamps," "10 stamps" etc.

Stope—Working above or below a level, where the mass of the ore body is broken or separated.

Stoping—Breaking the ore above or below a level. Overhand or Back Stoping is breaking it from the back of the drift; if from the Sole it is called Underhand Stoping.

Stratum—Plural Strata; A bed of earth or rock consisting usually of a series of layers.

Strike—Trend, Course; the extension of a lode on a horizontal line.

Stulls—Cross timbers at the foot of the stope.

Sublimation Theory—That idea which ascribes the filling of the fissures to material deposited by means of ascending steam or by condensation from a gaseous condition.

Sulphide—Sulphuret; Sulphur and a metal chemically united.

Sulphur--A mineral, non-metallic, insoluble in water, burns with a peculiarly suffocating smell.

Sulphuret—Sulphide; A combination of sulphur with another element.

Sump—The pit at the bottom of shift or its extension where water collects.

Syndicate---A number of persons not necessarily co-partners nor a corporation, but a combination formed for an especial occasion to carry on an agreed speculation or financial undertaking, the combination usually terminating with the completion of the enterprise.

Sylvanite---Native tellurium, sometimes called graphic tellurium.

Tackle--The windlass, the rope and the bucket.

Tailings--The refuse discharged from the tail or lower end of sluice or from any sort of workings.

Tellurium--A white, silvery, brittle substance, generally classed among metals. It is usually combined with gold, silver, lead and copper, Sp. gravity 6.65; at. wt. 128 Symbol Te.

Tin--A soft, white, very malleable metal; sp. gravity 7.2, fuses 442 deg. Fahr., at. wt. 117.7. Symbol Sn. Produced principally in England: 10,000 tons per annum.

Trachyte--A building stone; red and white, smetimes gray. Weighs about 140 pounds to the cubic foot.

Travertine--A building material similar in appearance to trachyte.

Tufa--A soft building stone that hardens upon exposure to the air.

Tributers--Miners who work properties on royalties but who work under the direction of the owners and hold no possession nor title as lessor.

Trouble--A fault.

Tunnel--A horizontal excavation starting at the surface.

Tut Work--Work paid for per the foot as distinguished from Tribute work.

Upcast--A ventilating shaft where the air must ascend.

Vein--Lode; ledge; reef; bed; an aggregation of mineral matter in fissures of rocks; the word has broader scope than lode, usually referring to non-metallic as well as metallic bodies; it is applied in working to the smaller seams which may thread the greater vein or lode. (see Vena and Veta.)

Vena--Branch of the Veta or main vein.

Veta--The main vein.

Vug---An ordinary Cavity; Pocket.

Wall---In referring to lodes; it is the plane of the Country where it touches the sides of the vein; in reference to workings ,it is the side of the level or drift.

Wheal---(old form Huel.) Cornish for mine; A pit or hole in the ground.

Whim---A machine with a revolving drum for raising the bucket

Whip---An arrangement for raising the bucket with the rope tackle and pulleys by horse power on a straight drive.

Winze---Shaft sunk from a level but not necessarily connecting two levels.

Zinc---Spelter; metal; bluish white; fuses 773 deg. Fahr.; generally found as a sulphide blende, or as a Carbonate (Calamine); atomic weight 65.2; specific gravity, 8.9.

Zone---A broad formation impregnated everywhere with mineral traversed by true fissures or lodes; the country containing lodes.

Relative Weights of Metals.

The weight of a piece of Yellow Pine being	1.	pound
Same size Cast Iron	16.	"
" " Steel	17.2	"
" " Copper	19.3	"
" " Brass	18.4	"
" " Lead	24.	"

To Protect Polished Steel or Iron from Rust.

Coat the surface with paraffine or steep the iron for a short time in solution of soda acidulated with hydrochloric acid.

Value of Rare Metals.

Silver, per pound Avoirdupois	$	7.50
Gold, " " "		301.75
Barium, " " "		1,000.
Calcium, " " "		1,800.
Cerium. " " "		1,920.
Chromium, " " "		3,200.
Gallium," " "		68,000.
Glucinum, " " "		4,000.

Aluminum—New Process.

The recent source of the product of aluminum from beauxite has entirely superseded its extract from clay. The process of extraction from clay is complicated and expensive, and its cost has caused it to be abandoned, while that of producing from beauxite is cheap. Beauxite is found in Alabama, Georgia and Tennessee, from which sources it is procured in quantity at low cost, and from which is now manufactured aluminum sufficient to supply the market.

Conflicting Location Laws.

The United States Mining Laws and the California State Mining Laws do not conflict. The former requires assessment work on a claim to the amount of $100 during the year, the latter $50 within sixty days. The object of the State law is to prevent the practice of relocating claims without doing the assessment work of $100 and to prevent locating numerous claims and holding them eleven months to the exclusion of others. Both the Federal and the State law must be complied with. The $50 worth of work done within sixty days may apply as a part and portion of the $100 assessment required by the Federal law. The balance may be done at any time during the year so as to conform to the following paragraph of Section 2324 Revised Statutes of the U. S.:

"Provided—That the period within which the work required to be done annually on all unpatented mineral claims shall commence on the first day of January succeeding the date of location of such claim and this section shall apply to all claims located since the tenth day of May, Anno Domini eighteen hundred and seventy-two."

Mining Partnership.

Co-owners who co-operate in the working of a mine or mining claim, sharing the expense and profits thereof, become thereby partners to the extent that all are liable for expenses incurred by anyone in operating or working the property. But if any co-owner refuses to contribute for working expenses, the others cannot compel him beyond his share of the annual assessment ($100) which the law requires (Dougherty vs. Creary, 30 Cal. 390).

Excerpts and Decisions.

MINING CLAIM IN TOWNSITE.—The fact that land on which discovery and location of a mining claim are made within patent limits of a town does not affect title of the locator where it was known prior to patent that mineral vein existed (Colorado App., 44 p. 69.)

CITIZENSHIP.—Citizenship of stockholders need not be shown to establish right to patent claim.

LIMIT TO NUMBER OF CLAIMS—There is no limitation to number of claims one person may hold by purchase or that may be included in a single patent or it seems in a single survey, showing only exterior boundaries and omitting all interior lines of the several smaller claims (104 U. S., 636 applied).

A VALID LOCATION OF A CLAIM.—The discovery must be within the limits of the claim (Colo. Sup., 45 p. 429).

DISCOVERY.—It is the finding of the mineral in the rock in place that constitutes discovery but it is not necessary that it be of such a nature that a practical miner would feel justified in following it up (Mont. 44, p. 979).

MUST OR MUST NOT RECORD.—If the rules of a mining district or state do not require recordation of location notices, there is no statute requiring recordation (16 Sup. Court, 282, 160 U. S. 305).

LOCATIONS, HOW MARKED.—Locations shall be distinctly marked so they can be readily traced on the ground (Rev. Stat. U. S., Sec. 2324.

AS AGENT.—A mining claim may be made by one person in the name of another.

An agent may locate a mining claim for his principal and make affidavit required by the Rev. Stat., Sec. 3104.

WORK BY ANOTHER.—Where adjoining claims are held in common, work for benefit of all may be done on any one of them in a given year to an amount required to be done by all (N. M. 42 p. 95).

WHAT IS NOT WORK.—Picking rock from walls of shaft and testing same from day to day to find paying rock is not "work" in the meaning of the law.

31

NOT ABANDONMENT.—A discoverer may transfer by parole an interest in his right and such transfer is not an abandonment of his right.

MINERAL ORES.—Deeds of "mineral ores" do not include granite (147 N. Y. 495).

OWNERS OF SURFACE land and minerals thereunder are not necessarily identical as to ownership or as to tenancy.

Some Nuggets.

"Sarah Sands"	Ballarat	130 pounds
"Blanche Barkly"	Kingower	145 pounds
"Welcome Nugget"	Ballarat	184 pounds
Byer & Haltman	Hill End, N. S. W.	640 pounds
"Welcome Stranger"	Mt. Moltgel	190 pounds
Oates & Nelson	Australia	$50,000
"Viscount of Canterbury"	Berlin, Victoria	$25,000
"Platypus"	Bedigo, Victoria	$7,500
"Ural"	Siberia	$24,000
"Tzar"	Siberia	$11,000
"Oliver Martin"	Camp Corona, Cal.	$22,700
"Monumental"	Sierra Buttes, Cal.	$9,800
"Hill"	Dutch Flat, Cal.	$12,300

Value of Ancient Money.

Gold, Shekel	132	Grains	$ 5.69
" Maneh	13,200	"	569.00
" Talent	1,320,000	"	56,900.00
" Daric or Dram (Persian)	128	"	5.52
Silver, Gerah	11	"	.02¼
" Beka	110	"	.26½
" Shekel	200	"	.53
" Maneh	13,200	"	32.00
" Talent	660,000	"	1,660.00
" Shekel (Maccabean)	220	"	.53
" "Piece of Money" (Stater)	220	"	.53
" Penny (Denarius)	58 6-7	"	.14
Copper, Shekel	528	"	.03—
" Mite	21	"	.00⅛
" Farthing (Quadrans)	42	"	.00¼
" " (Assarium)	84	"	.00½

Date of First Gold Excitement.

January 24, 1848, John W. Marshall found a piece of gold weighing 17 grains in a mill race at Sutter's Mill, Coloma, Eldorado County, California.

California Petroleum.

	Barrels.	Value.
1893	470,179	$ 608,092
1894	783,078	1,064,521
1895	1,245,339	1,000,235

The gross mineral product for 1895 was $23,000,000.

Gold Production of California.

1892	$12 571,000
1893	12,122,844
1894	13,923,281
1895	15,334,317
1896	14,004,108
1897	15,527,304
1898	17,625,959

THE PRODUCTION of gold in Australia for 1896 was 2,376,000 ounces. Sixty per cent of the gold product is from Victoria.

IN BRITISH COLUMBIA any miner or prospector before working in mines even for wages, must obtain a government license costing $5.

THE STATE MINERALOGIST of California shows that the average earning per capita in mining is about $1500, as against $1000. in manufacturing, and $300. in ranching. The number of miners is 19,508.

How Much per Day.

Judge Brantley of the District Court of Deer Lodge Coutny, Montana, recently decided where 23 days work was claimed, at $5, per day to hold a Claim, that the regular wages paid for such labor would hold, ie. $3. per day. The claimant therefore lost his claim.

33

An Opinion on the California Location Law.

BY THEODORE MARTIN, ESQ., OF THE LOS ANGELES BAR.

With all due respect to the learned Attorney General of the State of California, I cannot concur in his opinion, as given in the letter following this opinion. He holds that Section 3 of Statute of California, approved March 27, 1897, concerning the locating of mining claims, which requires that the locator must "within sixty days from the date of discovering of a vein or lode perform $50. worth of labor in developing his discovery", is in conflict with Section 2324 of the Revised Statutes of the United States and therefore null and void. The Section last cited as amended in 1880, makes it obligatory upon the locator to do $100.00 worth of improvement on his claim each year, after the year in which the claim is located until a patent is obtained; the Federal Law being silent as to work or improvement during the year in which the claim is located.

The case cited by the Attorney General, 60th Cal. 631, I do not consider in point, as the rule passed upon by our Supreme Court in that case was one requiring the miner to do some work on his claim every 60 days in order to hold his claim, but the $50. worth of labor demanded by Section 3 of this California Statute, is merely one of certain acts which the miner must do to perfect his location; thereafter no work or improvement whatever is required under the State Law. Under the laws of Arizona, Colorado Idaho, Montana, and other states, the miner must, within 60 or 90 days from the date of his discovery, sink a shaft upon his claim at least 10 feet deep on the vein. In Colorado the time in which this shaft must be sunk is sixty days from the date of discovery, this has been the law in the latter state for more than 20 years, and has been upheld by the highest Court in that state, and has been referred to with much approval by the United States Supreme Court in the case of Erhardt vs Boaro, 113 U. S., 1113, the opinion of the Court, which was delivered by Mr. Justice Field, who said in part "The statute of Colorado requires that the discoverer before a certificate of location is filed for record, shall, in addition to posting the notice mentioned at the point of discovery, sink upon the lode to the depth of at least 10 feet * * * the laws of the United States do not prescribe any time in which the excavations necessary to enable the locator to prepare and record a certificate shall be made. That is left to the legislation of the state, which, as we have stated, prescribes 60 days for the excavations upon the vein from the date of discovery".

In many instances the sinking of this shaft would cost less than $50., in some cases it would cost more than $100., depending wholly upon the character of the ground, hardness of rock, etc. If a state statute which requires the miner to do a certain amount of work in a certain manner is good, why is not the California statute good that requires the locator to make improvements of a certain value in the manner that may seem best to the one locating the claim?

I regard this California statute as being supplementary to the Federal statutes and not in conflict with them, and in my opinion those who wished to make legal locations of either lode or placer claims in this state, will do well to follow strictly the provisions of the California statute referred to herein.

[Since above was written The Superior Court of San Bernardino County, Cal., has decided that this statute is constitutional and valid. June 22, 1898.—Ed.]

March 28, 1899 this statute was repealed, and a new Bill passed but Gov. Gage would only sign the repeal at the last moment.

The Constitutionality of the California Law in Locating Claims.

THE U. S. SUPREME COURT AND OTHER AUTHORITIES DO NOT AGREE WITH THE FOLLOWING OPINION OF THE ATTORNEY GENERAL OF THIS STATE.

ATTORNEY-GENERAL'S OFFICE,
  STATE OF CALIFORNIA.

SAN FRANCISCO, CAL., June 29th 1897.

Los Angeles Chamber of Commerce,
  Los Angeles, Cal.

Gentlemen :—
  I am in receipt of your favor of recent date, enclosing a clipping from the Los Angeles Times, relative to the new mining law enacted by our last Legislature and suggesting that there is a conflict between such portions of that law as require a certain amount of assessment work upon mines located under the Federal laws to be done within a specified time, and the Federal laws relative to the same subject, and in which you request my opinion as to whether or not such a conflict exists.

35

By section 2324 of the Revised Statutes of the United States, it is required that not less than one hundred dollars worth of labor "shall be performed or improvements made during each year" upon each claim located after the 10th day of May, 1872, and until a patent has been issued for such a claim. By the provisions of section 3 of "An Act prescribing the manner of locating mining claims upon the public domain of the United States" etc approved March 27, 1897, (Stats. 1897, 214 et seq.,) it is provided, among other things, that "Within sixty days from the date of the discovery of a vein or lode, the discoverer must perform fifty dollars' worth of labor in developing his discovery," and by section 5 of the same Act it is provided that "The performance of such labor shall be deemed a necessary act in completing such location and a part thereof, and no part thereof shall inure to the benefit of any subsequent location."

It will thus be seen that there is an attempt on the part of the State to require at least fifty dollars worth of the location work to be done within a time less than that prescribed for the doing of the location work by the Federal statute. In the case of the Original Co. of the W. & K., etc. vs. The Winthrop Mining Co. 60 Cal., 631-2, the opinion of the Supreme Court of this State is as follows:

"We think that the Court erred in charging the jury that a locator of a mining claim must not only observe the law of Congress which requires that, ten dollars' worth of labor shall be performed or improvements made each year for each one hundred feet in length along the vein, until a patent shall have been issued therefor, but also the local regulation of the miners of the district, which require 'that work shall be done every sixty days on the claim.'

"According to the law of Congress, a locator would forfeit his claim if he did not each year perform work or make improvements of the value of ten dollars for each hundred feet of the vein. But by the local regulations, he would forfeit it if he did not perform some work on it every sixty days. It seems to us that there is a clear conflict between the law and the regulations. And if there is, it is conceded that the law must prevail."

I am of the opinion that the restriction attempted by the State mining law of 1897, above quoted, is of a character similar to the restriction attempted by the local regulations which were held in the case cited to be in conflict with the Federal laws. I am therefore of the opinion that the requirements of our statute as to the time within which assessment work must be done conflicts with the provisions of the Revised Statutes of the United States above referred to.

Respectfully,

W. F. Fitzgerald,

Attorney-General.

U. S. Mining Laws.

N. DEPARTMENT OF THE INTERIOR.
GENERAL LAND OFFICE,

WASHINGTON, D. C., March 14, 1898.

Registers and Receivers,
· United States Land Offices.

Gentlemen: Paragraph 53 of the Mining Regulations approved December 15, 1897, is hereby amended to read as follows:

The claimant at the time of the filing the application for patent, or at any time within the sixty days of publication, is required to file with the register, a certificate of the surveyor-general that not less than five hundred dollars' worth of labor has been expended or improvements made, by the applicant or his grantors, upon each location embraced in the application, or if the application embraces several locations held in common, that an amount equal to five hundred dollars for each location, has been so expended upon, and for the benefit of the entire group; that the plat filed by the claimant is correct; that the

37

field notes of the survey, as filed, furnish such an accurate description of the claim as will if incorporated in a patent serve to fully identify the premises and that such reference is made therein to natural objects or permanent monuments as will perpetuate and fix the locus thereof: Provided, That as to all applications for patent made and passed to entry before July 1, 1898, or which are by protests or adverse claims prevented from being passed to entry before that time, where the application embraces several locations held in common, proof of an expenditure of five hundred dollars upon the group will be sufficient and an expenditure of that amount need not be shown to have been made upon, or for the benefit of, each location embraced in the application.

Very respectfully,

BINGER HERMANN,
Commissioner.

Approved :

C. N. BLISS,
Secretary.

Montana.

Montana Mining Regulations 22 L. D., 624 were modified, paragraph 29 amended so as to read as follows; The claimant is then required to post a copy of the plat of such survey in a conspicous place upon the claim, together with notice of his intention to apply for a patent therefor. which notice will give the date of posting, the name of claimant, the name of the claim, the mining district, and the county; whether or not the location is of record and, if so, where the record may be found, giving the book and the page, the number of feet claimed along the vein and the presumed direction thereof; the number of feet claimed on the lode in each direction from the point of discovery, or other well defined place on the claim; the names of all adjoining and conflicting claims, or if none exist, the notice should so state.

According to the last decision of the department. the amendment of said paragraph will take effect June 1st. 1897 and all publications made or started prior to that date are to be treated in accordance with the former practice of the department.

Commissioner of the General Land Office.

Idaho.

A new law of Idaho provides that none but citizens of the United States may be employed as miners.

Idaho's new law for locations requires locator to put a post or monument at each corner and within 15 days make an excavation of not less than 100 cubic feet for purpose of prospecting.

Alaska.

The manner of locating mining claims, both lode and placer, in the Territory of Alaska is controlled by the statutes of the United States, just the same as in the other territories and states, subject to regulations as may be made by the Secretary of the Interior with the approval of the President, the miners of each mining district may make regulations not in conflict with the laws of the United States, governing the manner of recording amount of work necessary to hold a mining claim, subject however to the following requirements: The location must be distinctly marked on the ground so that its boundaries can be readily traced. All records of mining claims shall contain the name or names of the locators, the date of the location, and such a description of the claim or claims located by reference to some natural object or permanent monument, as will identify the claim. Lode claim must not exceed 1500 feet in length by 600 feet in width. In each year, beginning after the year in which the claim is located, $100. of work or improvements must be done on each claim.

A placer claim must not contain more than 20 acres, but 8 persons may locate 160 acres in one piece; the $100. of improvements must be performed as provided for lode claims, only that if 160 acres is located as above mentioned, $100. worth of improvements will be sufficient in each year to hold 160 acres; if a less number or even less than 20 acres be in one location, it will require $100. of improvements. This annual improvement is only required until patent is obtained. $500. of work or improvements must be performed before a patent can be obtained.

Klondyke.

Mining in the Klondyke and other districts on the Yukon River and its tributaries, which lie within the Canadian territory are of course subject to the laws of the Dominion of Canada; the following are the laws and rules in force at present in that locality.

Klondyke--Cont'd.

1189.

PRIVY COUNCIL—CANADA, AT THE GOVERNMENT HOUSE AT OTTAWA,
Friday the 21st day of May, 1897.

Present: His Excellency, The Governor General, In Council.

WHEREAS it is found necessary and expedient that certain amendments and additions should be made to the regulations governing "placer mining" established by order of Council of the 9th November, 1889; Therefore, His Excellency, in virtue of the provisions of "The Dominion Lands Act," Chapter 54 of the Revised Statutes of Canada, and by and with the advice of the Queens Privy Council for Canada, is pleased to order that the following regulations shall be and the same are hereby substituted for the governance of placer mining along the Yukon River and its tributaries in the Northwest territories in the room, place and stead of those regulations established by Order in Council of the 9th November, 1889.

(Sd)

JOHN J. McGEE,
Clerk of Privy Council.

To THE HONORABLE,
THE MINISTER OF THE INTERIOR.

Regulations Governing Placer Mining along the Yukon River and its Tributaries in the Northwest Territories.

DEFINITION OF TERMS.

"**BAR DIGGINGS**" shall mean any part of a river over which the water extends, when the water is in its flooded state, and which is not covered at low water. Mines on benches shall be known as "BENCH DIGGINGS" and shall for the purpose of defining the size of such claims be excepted from dry diggings.

"**DRY DIGGINGS**" shall mean any mine over which a river never extends.

"MINER" shall mean a male or female over the age of eighteen but not under that age.

"CLAIM" shall mean the personal right of property in a placer mine or diggings during the time for which the grant of such mine or diggings is made.

"LEGAL POST" shall mean a stake standing not less than four feet above the ground and squared on four sides for at least one foot from the top. Both sides so squared shall measure at least four inches across the face. It shall also mean any stump or tree cut off and squared or faced to the above height and size.

"CLOSE SEASON" shall mean the period of the year during which placer mining is generally suspended. The period to be fixed by the Gold Commissioner in whose district the claim is situated.

"LOCALITY" shall mean the territory along a river, (tributary of the Yukon), and its affluents.

"MINERAL" shall include all minerals whatsoever other than coal.

Nature and Size of Claims.

1. Bar diggings, a strip of land 100 feet wide at high water mark and thence extending into the river to its lowest water level,

2. The sides of a claim for bar digging shall be two parallel lines run as nearly as possible at right angles to the stream and shall be marked by four legal posts one at each end of the claim at or about high water mark, also one at each end of the claim at or about the edge of the water. One of the posts at high water mark shall be legibly marked with the name of the miner and the date upon which the claim was staked.

3. Dry diggings shall be 100 feet square and shall have placed at each of its four corners a legal post upon one of which shall be

legibly marked the name of the miner and the date upon which the claim was staked.

4. Creek and River claims shall be 100 feet long measured in the direction of the general course of the stream, and shall extend in width from base to base of the hill or bench on each side but when the hills or benches are less than 100 feet apart the claim may be 100 feet in depth. The sides of a claim shall be two parallel lines run as nearly as possible at right angles to the stream. The sides shall be marked with legal posts at or about the edge of the water and at the rear boundaries of the claim. One of the legal posts at the stream shall be legibly marked with the name of the miner and the date upon which the claim was staked.

5. Bench claims shall be 100 feet square.

6. In defining the size of claims they shall be measured horizontally irrespective of inequalities on the surface of the ground.

7. If any person or persons shall discover a new mine and such discovery shall be established to the satisfaction of the Gold Commissioner, a claim for bar diggings 200 feet in length may be granted. A new stratum or auriferous earth or gravel situated in a locality where the claims are abandoned shall for this purpose be deemed a new mine, although the same locality shall have been previously worked at a different level.

8. The forms of application for a grant for placer mining and the grant of the same shall be those contained in forms "H" and "I" in the schedule hereto.

9. A claim shall be recorded with the Gold Commissioner in whose district it is situated within three days after the location thereof if it is located within ten miles of the Commissioner's office. One extra day shall be allowed for making such record for every additional ten miles or fraction thereof.

10. In the event of the absence of the Gold Commissioner from his office, entry for a claim may be granted by any person whom he may appoint to perform his duties in his absence.

11. Entry shall not be granted for a claim which has not been staked by the applicant in person in the manner specified in these regulations. An affidavit that the claim was staked out by the applicant shall be embodied in form "H" of the schedule hereto.

12. An entry fee of $15.00 shall be charged the first year and an annual fee of $15 00 for each of the following years. This provision shall apply to locations for which entries have already been granted.

13. After the recording of a claim the removal of any post by the holder thereof or by any person acting in his behalf for the purpose of changing the boundaries of his claim shall act as a forfeiture of the claim.

14. The entry of every holder for a grant for placer mining must be renewed and his receipt relinquished and replaced every year. The entry fee being paid each year.

15. No miner shall receive a grant for more than one mining claim in the same locality, but the same miner may hold any number of claims by purchase, and any number of miners may unite to work their claims in common upon such terms as they may arrange, provided such agreement be registered with the Gold Commissioner and a fee of $5.00 paid for each registration.

16. Any miner or miners may sell, mortgage, or dispose of his or their claims, provided such disposal be registered with and a fee of $2.00 paid to the Gold Commissioner, who shall thereupon give the assignee a certificate in form "I" in the schedule hereto.

17. Every miner shall during the continuance of his grant have the exclusive right of entry upon his own claim, for the minerlike working thereof, and the construction of a residence thereon, and shall be entitled exclusively to all the proceeds realized therefrom; but he shall have no surface rights therein; and the Gold Commissioner may grant to the holders of adjacent claims such right of entry thereon as may be absolutely necessary for the working of their claims, upon such terms as may to him

seem reasonable. He may also grant permits to miners to cut timber thereon for their own use, upon payment of the dues prescribed by the regulations in that behalf.

18. Every miner shall be entitled to the use of so much of the water naturally flowing through or past his claim, and not already lawfully appropriated, as shall, in the opinion of the Gold Commissioner be necessary for the due working thereof; and shall be entitled to drain his own claim free of charge.

19. A claim shall be deemed to be abandoned and open to occupation and entry by any person when the same shall have remained unworked on working days by the grantee thereof or by some person on his behalf for the space of seventy-two hours, unless sickness or other reasonable cause be shown to the satisfaction of the Gold Commissioner or unless the grantee is absent on leave given by the Commissioner, and the Gold Commissioner upon obtaining evidence satisfactory to himself that this provision is not being complied with may cancel the entry given for claim.

20. If the land upon which a claim has been located is not the property of the Crown, it will be necessary for the person who applied for the entry to furnish proof that he has acquired from the owner of the land the surface rights before entry can be granted.

21. If the occupier of the lands has not received a patent therefor, the purchase money of the surface rights must be paid to the Crown and a patent of the surface rights will issue to the party who acquired the mining rights. The money so collected will either be refunded to the occupier of the land, when he is entitled to a patent therefor, or will be credited to him on account of payment for land.

22. When the party obtaining the mining rights to lands cannot make an arrangement with the owner thereof for the acquisition of the surface rights, it shall be lawful for him to give notice to the owner or his agent or the occupier to appoint an

arbitrator to act with another arbitrator named by him, in order to award the amount of compensation to which the owner or occupant shall be entitled. The notice mentioned in this section shall be according to the form to be obtained upon application fron the Gold Commissioner for the district in which the lands in question lie, and shall when practicable, be personally served on such owner, or his agent, if known, or occupant; and after reasonable efforts have been made to effect personal service, without success, then such notice shall be served by leaving it at, or sending by registered letter to, the last place of abode of the owner, agent or occupant. Such notice shall be served upon the owner, or agent, within a period to be fixed by the Gold Commissioner before the expiration of the time limited in such notice. If the proprietor refuses or declines to appoint an arbitrator, or when, for any other reason, no arbitrator is appointed by the proprietor in the time limited therefor in the notice provided for by this section, the Gold Commissioner for the district in which the lands in question lie, shall, on being satisfied by affidavit that such notice has come to the knowledge of such owner, agent or occupant, or that such owner, agent or occupant wilfully evades the service of such notice, or cannot be found, and that reasonable efforts have been made to effect such service, and that the notice was left at the last place of abode of such owner, agent or occupant, appoint an arbitrator on his behalf.

23. (a) All arbitrators appointed under the authority of these regulations shall be sworn before a Justice of the Peace to the impartial discharge of the duties assigned to them, and they shall forthwith proceed to estimate the reasonable damages which the owner or occupants of such lands, according to their several interests therein, shall sustain by reason of such prospecting and mining operations.

(b) In estimating such damages, the arbitrators shall determine the value of the land irrespectively of any enhancement thereof from the existence of minerals therein.

(c) In case such arbitrators cannot agree, they may select a third arbitrator, and when the two arbitrators cannot agree upon a third arbitrator the Gold Commissioner for the district in which the lands in question lie shall select such third arbitrator.

(d) The award of any two such arbitrators made in writing shall be final, and shall be filed with the Gold Commissioner for the district in which the lands lie.

If any cases arise for which no provision is made in these regulations, the provisions of the regulations governing the disposal of mineral lands other than coal lands approved by His Excellency the Governor in Council on the 9th of November, 1889, shall apply.

Arizona.

SECTION 1. Every notice of location of a mining claim shall contain: First, the name of the claim located; second, the name of the locator; third, the date of location; fourth, the number of feet in length of said claim and the number of feet claimed on each side of the centre of the discovery shaft, lengthwise of the claim; fifth, the general course of the lode, deposit or premises located; sixth, the locality of the claim with reference to some natural object, or permanent monument, as will identify the claim.

SEC. 2. All mining locations hereafter located, the certificate of location of which shall not contain: First, the name of the lode or premises; second, the name of the locator or locators; third, the date of location; fourth, the number of feet in length of said claim, and the number of feet claimed on each side of the center of the discovery shaft, lengthwise of the claim; fifth, the general course of the lode or premises, as near as may be; sixth, the locality of the claim with reference to some natural object or permanent monument, as will identify the claim, shall be void.

SEC. 3. Before filing such location certificate with the county recorder of the proper county, the discoverer shall locate his claim by: First, sinking a discovery shaft upon the premises so claimed, to a depth of at least ten feet from the lowest part of the rim of such shaft at the surface, and deeper if necessary, until there is shown by such work a lode deposit or mineral in place; second, by posting at the point of discovery on the surface, a plain sign or notice substantially conforming to the location certificate; third, by marking such claim or premises on the ground so that its boundaries can be readily traced.

SEC. 4. Such surface boundaries shall be marked by eight substantial posts, projecting at least three feet above the surface of the ground or by substantial stone monuments at least three feet high, to-wit: One at each corner of said claim, and one at the center of each end and side line thereof.

SEC. 5. Any open cut, cross cut, adit or tunnel, which shall be made as above provided for, as a part of the location of a mining claim, and which shall be equal in amount of work to a shaft ten feet deep and four feet wide by six feet long, and which shall cut a lode or mineral in place at the depth of ten feet from the surface, shall be equivalent, as a discovery work, to a shaft sunk from the surface.

SEC. 6. The discoverer shall have ninety days from the date of discovering the lode and the posting of the notice thereon to perform said discovery work thereon.

SEC. 7. If at any time the locator of any mining claim heretofore or hereafter located, or his assigns, shall learn that his original certificate was defective, or that the requirements of the law had not been complied with before filing, or shall be desirous of changing his surface boundaries or taking in any additional ground which is subject to location, or in case the original certificate was made prior to the passage of this law, and he shall be desirous of securing the benefits of this act, such

47

locator or his assigns, may file an amended certificate of location, subject to the provisions of this act regarding the making of new locations.

SEC. 8. The amount of assessment or representation work or improvements to be done or made during each year after the completion of the location as heretofore provided, and the time for doing the same, shall be as provided by the laws of the United States.

SEC. 9. Within three months after the expiration of the period of time fixed for the performance of annual labor or the making of improvements upon any mining claim or premises, the person on whose behalf such work or improvement was made, or some person for him, knowing the facts, may make and record in the office of the county recorder of the county wherein such claim is situate, an affidavit in substance as follows: (See Wolcott's Mining Blank No. 10.)

SEC. 10. Such affidavit, when so recorded, shall be prima facie evidence of the performance of such labor or the making of such improvements, and said original affidavit, after it has been recorded, or a certified copy of record of same shall be received as evidence accordingly by all the courts of this territory.

SEC. 11. The relocation of forfeited or abandoned lode claims shall only be made by sinking a new discovery shaft and fixing new boundaries in the same manner and to same extent as is required in making a new location; or the relocator may sink the original discovery shaft ten feet deeper than it was at date of commencement of such relocation, and shall erect new, or make the old monuments the same as originally required. In either case, a new location monument shall be erected and the location certificate shall state if the whole or any part of the new location is located as abandoned property.

DRAINAGE.—Whenever adjacent or contiguous mines, whether worked upon the same or separate lodes, have a common ingress or common drainage, they shall bear their proportionate share of such drainage expense to prevent the flowing of water upon neighboring mines. In case of failure to drain whereby occupants of adjacent or contiguous mines are compelled to provide for water flowing in from first-mentioned mine, parties in default shall pay their proportion of actual and necessary cost of providing for said water, to be recovered by action. Common interests may unite in draining such mines, as a corporation, with all the rights, incidents and liabilities of a body corporate so far as the same may be applicable. Failing to agree as above indicated, one or more of said parties, after reasonable notice to others interested, may drain, dividing and recovering by action the proportionate expense thereof. In an action to recover such expense, examination of the mines may be had before trial under order of court upon at least three days' notice; provided defendant has refused plaintiff or his agent the privilege to make said examination. These provisions do not apply to unopened or undeveloped mines.

PROBATE COURT.—Mines or interests therein belonging to estates of decedents may be sold by order of probate court having jurisdiction of the estate, upon petition by party in interest, and personal service on all persons interested in the estate of order to show cause, etc.

WATER RIGHTS.—The common-law doctrine of riparian rights is abolished. All rivers, creeks and streams of running water are public and applicable to the purposes of irrigation and mining. Rights in acequias, or irrigating canals, heretofore established shall not be disturbed, nor the course of such acequias be changed without consent of the proprietors of such established rights. Right to irrigate shall be preferable to all others, and shall not be obstructed or impeded by the erection of any dam, mill, machinery, or by any sluice or dyke, except for mining purposes or reduction of metals as hereinafter provided. When reduction works or other mining apparatus shall be placed upon lands previously held for agricultural purposes the holder thereof shall be entitled to a remuneration to be fixed by appraisement of damages.

EMINENT DOMAIN.—The right of eminent domain may be exercised in behalf of canals, ditches, flumes, acqueducts and pipes, for public transportation, supplying mines and farming neighborhoods with water, etc.; roads, tunnels, ditches, flumes, pipes and dumping places for working mines; also outlets, natural or otherwise, for the flow, deposit or conduct of tailings or refuse matter from mines; also, an occupancy in common by the owners or possessors of different mines of any place for the flow, deposit or conduct of tailings or refuse matter from their several mines.

British Columbia.

NEW PLACER LAW JUST PASSED BY THE ASSEMBLY.

The text of that portion of the act recently passed by the Assembly of British Columbia by which American miners are to be excluded from working placer mines in that province is as follows:

(1.) Every person who is not less than eighteen years of age, and is a British subject, shall be entitled to all the rights and privileges of a free miner under this act, and shall be considered a free miner under this act, upon taking out a free miner's certificate, as long as such certificate remains in force.

(2.) No joint stock company or corporation shall be entitled to take out a free miner's certificate unless the same has been incorporated, and not simply licensed or registered, under the laws of the province, and unless such company or corporation is authorized to take out a miner's license by the Lieutenant-Governor in Council. The word 'person' in this section shall include only such companies or corporations as aforesaid.

(3.) A miner's license taken out by any person not authorized so to do by this section shall be null and void.

(4.) This section shall not affect free miner's licenses issued before coming into force of this section, and in case any person or corporation not allowed under this section to take out a miner's license has, prior to the coming into force of this section, acquired any interest in any claim under the provisions of the 'Placer mining act,' such license may be renewed from time to time, but such renewed license shall not entitle the holder thereof to hold or acquire any interest in any claim under said 'Placer mining act,' except such interest so acquired prior to the coming into force of this section.

(5.) No free miner, after the coming into force of this section, shall hold any claim under said 'Placer mining act,' or any interest therein, as trustee or otherwise, for any person who is not a British subject, or for any corporation not authorized to take out a free miner's certificate as above provided.

Montana.

Any person a citizen of the United States, or one who has declared his intention to become such, who discovers a vein or lode bearing gold, silver, cinnabar, lead, tin, copper or other valuable deposits, or who discovers or locates a placer deposit of gold, or other deposit of minerals, including building stone limestone, marble, clay, sand, or other mineral substances having commercial value, may locate a claim upon such vein, lode or deposit, by defining the boundaries of the claim and by posting a notice of such location at the point of discovery. which notice must contain:

1. The name of the lode or claim.
2. The name of the locator or locators.
3. The date of location.
4. If a lode claim, (no lode claim can exceed 1,500 feet along

the vein by 600 feet) the number of linear feet claimed in length
along the course of the vein, each way from the point of discovery, with the width on each side of the center of the vein,
and the general course of the vein or lode as near as may be.

5. If a placer or millsite claim, the number of acres or
superficial feet claimed. (No placer claim can exceed twenty
acres in extent. No one millsite can exceed five acres in
extent, but each claim is entitled to one millsite. There is no
limit to the number of lode claims, or placer claims that one
locator may take up.)

Before the expiration of ninety days from the posting of
such notice upon the claim the locator or locators must sink a
discovery shaft upon the lode or claim, (millsites excepted) to
the depth of at least ten feet from the lowest part of the rim of
such shaft at the surface, or deeper, if necessary, to show a well-
defined crevice or valuable deposit. Its equivalent in work
must be done on placer claims. A cut, a cross cut or a tunnel
which cuts a lode at a depth of ten feet below the surface or an
open cut of at least ten feet in length along the lode from the
point where the lode may be in any manner discovered, is
equal to a discovery shaft. The locator, or locators, must define
the boundaries of the claim by marking a tree or rock in place, or
by setting a post or stone at each corner or angle of the claim.
When a post is used, it must be at least four inches square by
four feet six inches in length, set one foot in the ground with a
mound of earth or stone four feet in diameter by two feet in
height, around the post. When a stone is used, not a rock in
place, it must be at least six inches square and eighteen inches
in length, set two-thirds of its length in the ground; trees,
stakes or monuments must be so marked as to designate the
corners.

Within ninety days of the date of posting of the location
notice on the claim, there must be filed in the office of the
county clerk of the county in which the lode or claim is

situated, a declaratory statement which must contain:

1. The name of the lode or claim.
2. The name of the locator or locators.
3. The date of location and such description of the location of said claim with reference to some natural object or permanent monument as will identify the claim.
4. If a lode claim, the number of linear feet claimed in length along the course of the vein, each way from the point of discovery, with the width on each side of the center of the vein and the general course of the lode or vein as near as may be.
5. If a placer or millsite claim, the number of acres or superficial feet claimed.
6. The dimensions and location of the discovery shaft or its equivalent sunk upon lode or placer claims.
7. The location and description of each corner with the markings thereon.

Such declaratory statements must be verified by the oath of one of the locators or officer of any corporation locating the same.

The owner of the lode or placer claim, who performs or causes to be performed the annual work or makes the improvements required by the laws of the United States, in order to prevent the forfeiture of the claim, may within twenty days after the annual work, file in the office of the county clerk of the county within which the claim is situated, an affidavit of his own, or an affidavit of the person who performed such work, showing:

1. The name of the claim and where situated.
2. The number of days' work done and the character and the value of the improvements placed thereon.
3. The date of performing such work.
4. At whose instance the work or labor was done.
5. The actual amount paid for the work or improvements, by whom paid, when the same was not done by the owner.

The relocation of an abandoned lode or placer claim must be made by sinking a new discovery shaft and fixing new boundaries in the same manner as if it were an original location, or the relocator may sink the original discovery shaft ten feet deeper, in which case the declaratory statement must give the depth and dimensions of the original discovery shaft at the date of such relocation.

Nevada.

Mining claims are located and held by virtue of the laws of the United States and local regulations thereby authorized. There is no state regulation in this respect, except (1) in case of proceedings against delinquent co-owners under the United State statutes. The moving party must, within thirty days after the time the title vests in him, have recorded in the office of the county recorder a copy of the notice given, with an affidavit of service, if personal, or an affidavit of publication, by the publisher or his clerk, when published, together with his own affidavit that the parties proceeded against have not paid their share of expenditure, or performed their share of labor. Such record or a copy thereof is prima facie evidence of the facts therein stated. (2) An affidavit of annual labor and expenditure made before the mining recorder of the district and recorded with him his prima facie evidence of the facts stated therein.

The right of eminent domain may be exercised in favor of mining, milling, smelting or other reduction of ores.

Three or more persons, owning a majority interest in any mining claim, may form themselves into an association or corporation for the purpose of working the same, and may sue any one owning with them, but not a member of such association or incorporation, for his pro rata share of the expense of working the same, without previous notice or demand.

54

Mining corporations may be compelled to allow stockholders to visit and examine the mines. Mining corporations may consolidate. In any mining district embracing a county seat, the county recorder shall be ex officio mining recorder. Mining recorders shall transmit copies of their records to the county recorder.

By act approved March 16th, A. D , 1897, it is enacted by the legislature, that the locator or locators shall, within ninety days of posting notice, sink a discovery shaft of ten feet in depth, or its equivalent in cuts or tunnels, and shall record his claim with the mining recorder and the county recorder where his claim is situated, which certificate of location for record shall contain, in addition to the requirements of the United States laws, the location and description of the work done on the claim, and the location and description of each corner post or monument with the markings thereon.

New Mexico.

Location must be distinctly marked on the ground, so that its boundaries may be readily traced. Written notice of location must be posted at some conspicuous place on the claim, and must contain a description thereof by reference to some natural object or permanent monument. A copy of this notice must be recorded in county clerk's office within three months after date of location.

The value of a day's labor is fixed at $4, or 8 hours of labor actually performed.

Locators must sink a discovery shaft, ten feet deep from lowest part of rim at surface, and expose mineral in place, before filing location notice, and within ninety days from date of location. Upon failure so to do, original locator is not permitted, under penalty, to relocate the claim or any part of it, during ninety days from the date first location expired; and affidavit setting out the details of such labor, must be filed within sixty days after completion, with the county recorder. No locator can have benefit of work done prior to his location. Changing location notice is punishable by fine or imprisonment or both, but amended location notices may be posted and filed. One hundred and twenty days from date of location are allowed for the statutory marking of surface boundaries, requirement being eight substantial posts or stone monuments at least three feet above the surface, at corners and at the centers of end and side lines, all marked with name and direction.

Where mine is under lien, the lien-holder has right of entry to do the annual assessment work, if owner neglects same, and a penalty attaches for any obstruction of that right. The cost of such assessment work is made an additional lien, following original lien as to tenor and effect. A stockholder in a mining corporation has right to entry to mine, and inspection of work, under penalty to officer or agent refusing to allow such entry. Thirty days' notice required to terminate an oral mining lease, except when damage is being done to property. Mine-owners have right of eminent domain for tramway or railway to transport ore to reduction works.

Ore purchasers and reducers must keep a detailed record of all ore received, with name of mine, person, etc. Under regulations, any party from whom ore has been stolen may have access to these books. Larceny of ore and knowing purchase thereof are made felonies.

False and malicious statement as to title, or knowingly making false claim or setting up a false lien, with a view to defeating sale of mining property, are felonies. It is a misdemeanor to tear down or change monuments, or remove or alter notices.

Oregon.

The constitution provides that no Chinaman not a resident of the state at the adoption thereof shall hold any mining claim or work any mining claim.

Any person or company establishing a lode claim is allowed to possess the land or vein for fifteen hundred feet in length and three hundred on each side. The discoverer is allowed an additional claim. Claim is established by posting a notice, good for thirty days, and if recorded before that time will hold claim till the first day of January next following the location thereof.

Within one year after the 1st day of January next following the location each claim must be worked to the amount of $100. Failure to do such work forfeits claim. Where several claims are held by one person or company all the work for all the claims may be performed on one. Upon filing the affidavit of one of the owners and those of two disinterested persons to the effect that such labor has been performed, such claims will thereafter be considered real estate and the title shall vest in the holders against all others save the government of the United States. Miners are empowered to make local laws in relation to water-rights, placer claims and town lots, in mining camps.

Ditches and flumes used for mining are declared real estate. Failure to use for one year after abandonment or removal from the state with intent to change residence and remaining absent one year, without exercising ownership over ditch, flume or water-right for mining, forfeits the claim to same. The laws relative to sale and transfer of real estate apply to ditches and flumes. Interest in placer mining claims may be conveyed by bill of sale and delivery of possession as in the case of sale of personal property.

South Dakota.

SIZE.—Mining claims shall not exceed fifteen hundred feet along the vein by one hundred and fifty feet on each side of the center thereof.

RECORD.—The discoverer of a lode shall, within sixty days from the date of discovery, record his claim in the office of the register of deeds of the county in which such lode is situated by a location certificate which shall contain:

1.   The name of the lode.

2.   The name of the locator or locators.

3.   The date of location.

4.   The number of feet in length claimed on each side of the discovery shaft.

5.   The number of feet in width claimed on each side of the claim or lode.

6.   The general course of the lode as near as may be.

Any location certificate which does not contain the foregoing requirements and such description as shall identify the claim with reasonable certainty shall be void.

MANNER OF LOCATION.—1.   Before filing such location certificate, the discoverer shall first sink a discovery shaft sufficient to show a well-defined mineral vein or lode, within sixty days from the time of the uncovering of the lode.

2   By posting at the point of discovery on the surface a plain sign, or notice, containing the first five requisites of the location certificate above given.

3.   By marking the surface boundaries of the claim by eight substantial posts hewed or blazed on the side or sides facing the claim and plainly marked with the name of the lode, and the corner, end or side of the claim that they respectively represent, and sunk in the ground, or, when necessary, in a monument of stone, to-wit: One at each corner and one at the center of each side-line and one at each end of the lode.

Utah.

LEASE OF STATE MINERAL LANDS.—State mineral lands may be leased for the purpose of obtaining therefrom such mineral, and conditioned upon payment of royalty upon product determined by state board of land commissioners.

EXTENT OF GROUND OPEN FOR LOCATION.—Locator may claim fifteen hundred feet along vein or lode and three hundred on each side of middle of vein or lode at surface except where adverse rights render less width necessary. End lines must be parallel. (Laws of 1897, page 57.)

LOCATION.—No location shall be made until discovery of vein or lode within limits of claim.

HOW LOCATED.—Locator, at time of discovery of vein or lode, must erect monument at discovery and post notice of location thereon containing:

1. Name of claim.
2. Name of locator.
3. Date of location.
4. Number of linear feet in length along vein, if lode claim, each way from discovery, with width on each side of center of vein and general course of vein and description of claim located by reference to some natural object, etc.
5. If placer or mill-site claim, number of superficial feet or acres and description of claim located by reference to some natural object, etc.

Within thirty days of date of discovery locator must mark boundaries of claim by monuments in each corner or angle, with name of claim and corner or angle represented.

MONUMENTS.—Monuments must be of such material and form as will readily give notice. When trees, must be hewn so as to attract attention, and trees and posts must be hewn and marked on side facing discovery and must be four inches in diameter. Monuments must be at least four feet high. Must be kept in state of preservation so as to give notice.

RECORDING.—Within thirty days from date of posting notice of location on claim locator must file copy in office of county recorder in county where claim is. Recording fee, $1.

ASSESSMENT WORK.—Within ninety days of posting location notice locator must do at least $50 worth of work. Work done for group at one point, notice must be posted at discovery point of each claim showing where work is being done.

Owner who has had annual labor performed required by United States to prevent forfeiture, must during year or within thirty days after completion of work, if completed after year, file in county recorder's office affidavit of persons doing such work showing:

1. Name of claim and where situated.

2. Number of days' work done and character and value of improvements.

3. Dates of performing said labor, etc., and number of cubic feet of earth, etc., removed.

4. At whose request work done.

5. Actual amount and by whom paid.

DISTRICT RULES AND REGULATIONS.—County recorder must record mining rules and regulations of mining districts.

EVIDENCE.—Certified copies of notice of location and mining district rules and regulations and affidavits of work, etc , recorded in county recorder's office, are prima facie evidence.

In actions respecting mining claims proof must be admitted of the customs, usages or regulations established and in force at the bar diggings or camp embracing such claim; and such customs, usages or regulations, when not in conflict with the laws of this state, or of the United States, must govern the decision of the action.

HOURS.—It is a misdemeanor for a person to work more than eight hours per day in an under-ground mine or smelter or other ore reduction works. except in case of emergency.

North Dakota.

LOCATION AND SIZE OF CLAIM.—Length of lode claims may equal but shall not exceed fifteen hundred feet; width shall not exceed one hundred and fifty feet each side of the center of the vein. Any county may by majority vote at a general election make a greater width, not to exceed three hundred feet each side of center, or less, but not less than twenty-five feet each side of center.

The discoverer of a lode must within sixty days from discovery record his claim in the office of the register of deeds of the county in which the lode is located. The location certificate must show the name of lode, name of locator, date of location, number of feet in length, number of feet in width claimed and general course of lode.

Before filing certificate the discoverer must locate claim by sinking discovery shaft, and post on surface notice containing name of lode and other particulars as required in certificate, and must mark surface boundaries of claim.

Surface boundaries must be marked by posts, set one at each corner and one in the middle of each side and end, marked on side next to claim with the name of lode, and the corner, end or side they respectively represent.

The discoverer shall have sixty days from the time of discovery of lode to sink a discovery shaft.

The location certificate shall include all surface ground within the surface lines thereof, and all lodes and ledges throughout their entire depth, the top or apex of which lies inside such lines extended vertically, with such parts of all lodes or ledges as continue by dip beyond the side-lines of the claim, but shall not include any portion of such lode or ledges beyond the end-line of the claim, nor beyond the side-lines except by dip of the lode.

When the right to mine is separate from the ownership or right of occupancy of the surface, the owner or occupant may demand satisfactory security, and if refused may enjoin the miner.

If locator deems the original certificate defective, he may file an amended certificate, provided it does not conflict with existing rights. Relocation does not preclude the locator from proving title under his previous location.

To hold possession of a mining claim $100 worth of work must be done or improvements made each year.

Relocation of abandoned claims shall be by new discovery shaft and fixing new boundaries, and the location certificate must state that the whole or part of the new location is on abandoned property.

No location certificate shall contain more than one location, whether made by one or more locators.

Washington.

LOCATION AND POSSESSION OF MINING LODES.—All mining claims shall be governed by law in force at time of location.

Mining claims located after February 2, 1888, upon any vein or lode, etc. (whether located by one or more persons), shall not exceed fifteen hundred feet in length along the vein, and three hundred on each side of the middle of the vein at the surface, but no location shall be made until the discovery of the vein or lode within the limits of the claim located.

RIGHTS OF LOCATION.—The locators of all mining claims on any mineral vein, lode or ledge on the public domain and their heirs and assigns (as long as they comply with the laws in relation thereto) shall have exclusive right to possession and use of all the surface included in the location, and all veins, lodes and ledges throughout their entire depth, and the top or apex of which lies within the surface line of their location extending downward vertically, although they may so far depart from the perpendicular as to extend outside of the vertical side line of the surface location.

RULES.—The miners of each mining district make rules an regulations governing location and amount of work necessary to hold possession not in conflict with the laws of the United States or this state, but on each claim one hundred dollars' ($100) worth of work must be done in each year. First year shall date from date of location. Failure to comply shall work forfeiture and claim may be relocated.

RECORDER.—Miners of each district may elect a recorder. Recorder when elected shall record all notices, transfers, bonds, conveyances and assignments of mining claims within the district. Such records declared to be public records and shall have same effect as to notice, etc., as the records of deeds and mortgages in this state. Recorder shall hold office for one year and until successor is elected, shall file oath with county auditor shall be certifying officer; fees shall be same as county auditor When vacancy in office, records shall be transmitted to county auditor and auditor shall keep such records as part of the records of his office, in districts where there is no mining recorder. Notices of location, etc., and other instruments shall be recorded in county auditor's office within thirty days after execution thereof. All records made prior to February, 1888, validated.

The governor appoints two coal mine inspectors for a term of four years. Inspectors have power to close any mine worked contrary to law; they are to proceed by injunction without bond.

Openings in mines worked by shaft, stope or drift must have at least two openings separated by natural strata by a distance of not less than 100 feet, provided twenty-four persons may be employed before the second opening is reached. The second opening must be made without delay.

Wyoming.

LODE AND PLACER CLAIMS.—In any mining district the miners may meet and organize and elect a recorder and make regulations, not in conflict with the laws of the United States or this state, governing the location, manner of recording and amount of annual work necessary to hold possession, subject to the following requirements:

1. Any five miners owning in part or in whole claims within the proposed district shall give at least three written notices of a meeting called by them for organizing such district.

2. The meeting must be attended by at least ten persons, owning in part or in whole claims within the proposed district.

3. The recorder elected shall hold office until his successor is elected and qualified; he shall give bonds for at least $1,000, which shall be approved by the probate judge, and filed in the office of the county clerk.

4. When a district is once organized it cannot be subdivided, except in accordance with local laws of the district, or by action of the legislature. In case of abandonment the recorder shall deposit all records pertaining to his office in the office of the register of deeds of the county.

5. Each mining district may regulate the fees for recording certificates and other instruments.

The laws and records of each mining district shall be filed with the county register of deeds.

MINING WATER RIGHTS.—Any person mining or milling in the state shall have the right to bring water from the mines or natural water-courses as their business interests may require, provided it shall not infringe on vested rights.

RIGHTS OF WAY.—All mining claims shall be subject to the right of way of any ditch or flume for mining purposes, or of any tramway, pack trail or wagon road across such claim or property; provided, such right of way shall not be exercised against such property without the consent of the owner, except in condemnation, as in the case of land taken for public highways. The owner of the surface property may demand satisfactory security from the miner, which, if refused, will give the right to said occupant of the surface to enjoin miner from working such mine.

RELOCATIONS.—When there is error in the original location certificate, or where it is desired to change the surface boundaries of the claim, such locator may file an additional location certificate in compliance with and subject to this act, provided such relocation shall not infringe upon the rights of others.

SIZE OF CLAIM.—The length of any mining claim located within the state shall not exceed fifteen hundred feet horizontally along such vein. The width shall not exceed three hundred feet on each side of the discovery shaft. A discoverer of a mineral vein, shall, within ninety days, record such claim with the recorder of the mining district if such district be organized, and shall within one hundred and twenty days record the same with the county clerk and ex-officio register of deeds by location certificate, which shall contain the following facts: 1. The name of the lode claim; 2. The name or names of the locator or locators; 3. The date of location; 4. The length and general course of the vein as far as it is known; 5. The amount of the surface ground claimed on either side; 6. A description of the claim by such designation of fixed objects as shall identify the claim beyond question.

DISCOVERY RIGHTS.—The discoverer of any mineral vein shall have a period of one hundred and twenty days in which to sink a discovery shaft. A discoverer of any placer claim shall, within thirty days, record such claim with the recorder of the mining district, if such district be organized, and shall, within ninety days, cause to be recorded such claim with the recorder of deeds of the county by a location certificate, which shall contain: 1. The name of the claim, designating it as a placer claim; 2. The name of the locator; 3. The date of location; 4. The number of feet or acres thus claimed; 5. A description of the claim by such designation of natural or fixed objects as shall identify it.

MISDEMEANOR.—Any person who shall unlawfully destroy any mining property shall be guilty of a misdemeanor and upon conviction thereof shall be fined a penal sum of money not less than $50 nor more than $1,000, or be imprisoned not less than thirty days nor more than one year, or both.

FRAUD—Any person who shall engage in any swindling, in relation to any mine or mining property, designing to cheat and deceive others for the purpose of gain, shall be guilty of a felony, and upon conviction thereof shall be fined any penal sum of not less than $50 nor more than $5,000 or imprisoned in the penitentiary for not less than 30 days nor more than 3 years, or both.

PROTECTION OF SHAFTS.—Any persons who have sunk mining-shafts upon any mining claim shall forthwith secure such shafts and openings against the injury of live stock running at large upon public domain, by covering them in a manner to render them safe, or by making a strong fence around such shaft or openings aforesaid. Any persons who shall fail to comply with this section shall be guilty of a misdemeanor and, upon conviction, shall be liable for damages sustained by loss of live stock thereby.

PATENTS FOR PLACER CLAIMS.—When any person has held and worked his claim in conformity with the laws of this state and the regulations of the mining district for five successive years after the 1st day of January succeeding the date of location, he shall be entitled to proceed to obtaining a patent for his claim from the United States without performing further work.

Coal mines are not included in this act.

RELOCATIONS.—No location certificate shall contain more than one claim or location. Where there is collusion for the purpose of obtaining possession of any mineral claim then in the actual possession of another, by force, threats or stealth, and they shall proceed to carry out such purpose, such persons so engaging shall be guilty of a misdemeanor and upon conviction shall be fined a penal sum not exceeding $25, and be imprisoned in the county jail for not less than sixty days nor more than six months. [See page 65.]

Arizona.

March 3rd, 1899.—Be it enacted by the Legislative Assembly of the Territory of Arizona:

Section 1. That act No. 68 of the Nineteenth Legislative Assembly of the Territory of Arizona, approved March 18, 1897, be amended to read as follows:

Sec. 2 The regents of the University of Arizona shall charge for assaying ores taken from deposits and mines within the Territory of Arizona $1 for each assay producing gold and silver, and $2 for each assay producing gold, silver and copper, and $2.50 for assaying ores showing more than three metals; that the maximum rate for an assay shall be $2.50 and the minimum rate for an assay shall be $1.

Sec. 3. There shall be a uniform fee of $1.50 charged by each County Recorder in the Territory of Arizona for recording each notice of location of a mining claim, including certificate of work done to comply with the law regarding locations; the said $1.50 to be in full for filing, the same under seal.

MINING CORPORATIONS —Any number of persons may associate themselves together and become incorporated for the transaction of any lawful business. Articles of incorporation must contain:

1. Names of corporators, name of corporation and principal place of transacting business. 2. General nature of the business proposed to be transacted. 3. Amount of capital stock authorized and times when and conditions upon which it is to be paid in. 4. The time of commencement and termination of corporation. 5. By what officers or persons affairs of corporation are to be conducted and times at which they are to be elected. 6. Highest amount of indebtedness or liability to which the corporation is at any time to subject itself. 7. Whether private property is to be exempt from corporate debts. Unless so exempted stockholders are liable for debts of the corporation, in the proportion which their stocks bear to the whole capital stock.

Colorado.

ANNUAL LABOR.—Annual labor, commonly called "assessment," was required by district rules prior to May 10, 1872. Since that time state legislation agrees with the act of congress. One hundred dollars' worth of labor must be performed or improvements made on each claim during each calendar year. (R. S., Sec. 2324; A. C., Jan. 22, 1880) Within six months thereafter, the person for whose benefit the same was performed may file with recorder of the county wherein the mine is situated an affidavit showing performance of the same, and describing lode and stating at whose expense same was performed. This affidavit or a certified copy of same becomes prima facie evidence of the performance of such labor or making such improvements. (S. L , 1880, p. 261; M. A. S., Sec. 3161.) A neglect to file such affidavit does not of itself leave a claim open to relocation.

LODES.—Lodes cannot exceed fifteen hundred feet in length. In Gilpin, Clear Creek, Boulder and Summit counties the width is one hundred and fifty feet and in all other counties three hundred feet, which width is to be evenly distributed on each side of the center of the vein or crevice. Under the decisions in this state it seems that the lode should be in place in the discovery shaft, but the discovery shaft need not be at the point where the lode was first discovered or disclosed. Each claim must have a separate discovery shaft. Known lodes within limits of a placer are excluded by the patent unless the lode belongs to claimant and is especially designated in the appli_cation. Where lodes cross or intersect, the one with prior title is entitled to the ore or mineral contained in the space of intersection, but subsequent location has a right of way through the intersection for the purpose of mining.

APEX AND DIP.—The location or location certificate of any lode claim shall be construed to include all the surface ground within the surface lines thereof and all lodes and ledges throughout their entire depth, the top or apex of which lies inside of such lines extended downward, vertically, with such parts of all lodes or ledges as continue by dip beyond the side lines of the claim, but shall not include any portion of such lode or ledges beyond the end lines of the claim or the end lines continued, whether by dip or otherwise, or beyond the side lines in any other manner than by the dip of the lode. (G. S., Sec. 2405.)

If the top or apex of the lode in its longitudinal course extends beyond the exterior lines of the claim at any point of the surface or as extended vertically downward, such lode may not be followed in its longitudinal course beyond the point where it is intersected by the exterior lines. (G. S. Sec. 2406.)

LOCATION.—No location of a mining claim shall be made until the discovery of the vein or lode within the limits of the claim located. The discoverer of a lode shall, within three months from the date of discovery, record his claim in the office of the recorder of the county in which such claim is situated, by a location certificate which shall contain, first, the name of the lode; second, the name of the locator; third, the date of location; fourth, the number of feet in length claimed on each side of the center of the discovery shaft; fifth, the general course of the lode as near as may be. (G. S., Sec. 2399; M. A. S., Sec. 3150.)

Before filing such location certificate the discover shall locate his claim by: First, sinking a discovery shaft upon the lode to a depth of at least ten feet from the lowest part of rim of such shaft at the surface, or deeper if necessary to show a well-defined crevice; second, by posting at the point of discovery at the surface a plain sign or notice containing the name of the lode, the name of the locator and the date of discovery. (G. S. Sec. 2401; M. A. S., Sec. 3152.)

Such surface boundaries shall be marked by six subtantial posts hewn or marked on the side or sides which are in toward the claim, and sunk in the ground, to-wit: One at each corner and one at the center of each side line. (G. S., Sec 2402; M. A. S., Sec. 3153.)

Any open cut, cross cut or tunnel which shall cut a lode at the depth of ten feet below the surface shall hold such lode the same as if a discovery shaft were sunk thereon, or an adit of at least ten feet in along the lode shall be equivalent to a discovery shaft. (G. S., Sec. 2403; M. A. S., Sec. 3154.)

The discoverer shall have sixty days from the time of uncovering or disclosing a lode to sink a discovery shaft thereon. The discovery shaft must be sunk upon unoccupied public land, that is to say, it must be outside of the lines of any patent or other valid location, and there must be a separate discovery for each claim. Where one lode crosses, runs into or unites with any other lodes, priority of title shall determine the rights to all ore or mineral contained within the space of intersection. If at any time the locator of any mining claim heretofore or hereafter located, or his assigns, shall apprehend that his original location certificate was defective, erroneous, or that the requirements of the law had not been complied with before filing, and shall be desirous of changing the surface boundaries or taking in any part of an over-lapping claim which has been abandoned, he may file an additional certificate, provided such relocation does not interfere with existing rights of others at the time of such relocation. (G. S., Sec. 2409; M. A. S., Sec. 3160.)

An abandoned lode claim may be relocated by sinking a new discovery shaft or sinking the original shaft ten feet deeper, and the erection of new boundaries and new location stakes, and the certificate shall state that the same has been located as abandoned property. (G. S., Sec. 2411; M. A. S., Sec. 3162.)

PLACER.—Stone quarries, oil land, kaolin, borax beds and asphaltum may be located as placers. A placer location must have a name. As to requirements of certificate see "Location."

The discoverer of a placer claim shall, within thirty days from the date of discovery, record his claim in the office of the recorder of the county in which claim is situated, by a location certificate which shall contain, first, the name of the claim, designating it as a placer claim; second, the name of the locator;

third; the date of location; fourth, the number of acres or feet claimed; fifth, a description of the claim by such reference to natural objects or permanent monuments as shall identify the claim.

Before filing such location certificate the discoverer shall locate his claim, first, by posting upon his claim a plain sign or notice containing the name of the claim, the name of the locator, the date of discovery and the number of acres or feet claimed; second, by marking the surface boundaries with substantial posts sunk in the ground, to-wit, one at each angle of the claim. It will be noted that the notice on stake must contain the date of discovery while the record must contain the date of location. See also "Lodes," Placer," "Apex."

TUNNEL —A territorial act in 1861 gave the right to locate and record tunnel sites with right to two hundred and fifty feet each way from said tunnel on each lode discovered, and such tunnel has a right of way through all lodes which may lie in its course. This act conflicts with the congressional acts, and is probably inoperative in part, but the grant of a right of way relieves the tunnel owner from liability for a technical trespass.

A recent act (S. L., 1897, p. 181) provides that any person having a tunnel, the mouth of which is upon his own ground, shall have the right to drive the same through and across any patented or located claims in front of the mouth of said tunnel, but not to follow the veins of others. Owners of intersected claims have the right to enter tunnel, without process of law, to inspect and survey, and refusal to permit the same or natural drainage, forfeits all tunnel rights. The ore extracted from the intersected veins belong to the vein owner. The burden of proof as to right to work a vein disclosed in a tunnel is on the tunnel owner.

71

Idaho.

WIDTH OF CLAIMS.—Mining claims hereafter located upon veins or lodes of quartz or other rock in place, or any metals or other valuable deposits, may extend to three hundred feet on each side of the middle of the vein or lode. The locator of any lode or mining claim must at the time of making the location place a substantial stake, post or monument, not less than four inches in diameter, at each end of the ground claimed, as near as practicable to the middle, and also a similar mark at each corner of the location, such marks to be at least four feet high and must be marked distinctly with the name and location of the claim.

NOTICE.—The notice of location must be conspicuously attached to one of said center end posts so that it may be easily read, or it must be posted in like manner at the point of discovery. The notice must contain the date of location, names of locators, name of claim, ledge or lode and quantity in feet claimed along the ledge or lode, the width claimed from the middle of the vein, and must also give such description of the locality by reference to natural landmarks as to render the situation of the same reasonably certain notice itself.

PLACER.—Placer claims may be located under like circumstances and conditions and upon similar proceeding as far as applicable to those provided in the case of lode claims, but must be recorded within thirty days from date of location.

RECORDING.—Every claim must be recorded within fifteen days from the time of posting the notice, in the district in which the claim is located, or at the nearest office. For the convenience of prospectors and locators the county recorders of the several counties must appoint a deputy at any place where they deem it necessary, and in all places more than ten miles distant from the existing office whenever ten or more mining locators interested petition for such appointment. Upon failure to make such appointment for ten days after receipt of petition the resident miners may temporarily appoint one of their own number to act as recorder, and his record shall be as valid as though made by deputy; provided, that whenever the recorder appoints a deputy for that district the authority of the person elected by the resident miners ceases. At the time of presenting a notice for record, or within five days thereafter, one of the locators named in the same must make and subscribe an affidavit in writing on or attached to the notice which must contain the name of the lode, ledge or claim, and must state that the claim therein described or any part thereof has not before been located according to the law of the United States in this state, or if so located has been abandoned or forfeited by reason of the failure of the locators to comply with the law.

How Recorded.—The notice herein required to be recorded is substantially the same as the notice placed upon the claim. It must be recorded by the deputy appointed by the district recorder or the person elected for that purpose (when the legal fee is tendered), in the book to be kept for that purpose. Said book must be indexed with the names of all locators arranged in alphabetical order. The fee to be tendered for making such record, administering the oath and certifying the same, and for indexing the names occurring on the notice, and to include recording of the notice by the recorder, is $2, which fee must be equally divided between the recorder and the deputy, and no other or additional sum of money must be demanded or received by either of them for any services connected with the recording of any location notice made pursuant to the requirements of this state.

· Right of Way—The owner, locator or occupant of a mining claim may have and acquire a right of way for ingress and egress when necessary in working such mining claim over and across the lands or mining claims of others. When any mine or mining claim is so situated that for the convenience and enjoyment of the same a road, railroad or tramway therefrom, or a ditch or canal to convey water thereto, or a ditch, flume, cut or tunnel to convey water or tailings therefrom, or a tunnel or shaft may be required for the better workings thereof, which road, railroad, tramway, ditch, canal, flume or tunnel may require the use or occupancy of lands owned, occupied or possessed by others, the owner, claimant or occupant of the mine or mining claim first mentioned is entitled to a right of way and to enter into possession for such uses and privileges. For such purposes a road, railroad, tramway, ditch, canal, flume or tunnel, in, upon, through and across such other lands or mining claims may be constructed upon compliance with the following provisions: When the owner, claimant or occupant of any mine or mining claim desires the right of way above mentioned and which cannot be acquired by agreement with owner of lands or claims over, under, across or upon which he seeks to establish this way, he may present to the judge of the district court within and for the county in which such right of way or some part thereof sought to be enforced is situated a petition that such right of way be awarded him. Such petition must be verified and contain a particular description of the nature and extent of the rights sought, a description of the mine or claim of petitioner and the claim or lands to be affected by such right, with the names of the owners or occupants thereof.

WATER RIGHTS.—The right to the use of running water may be acquired by appropriation, if it be for any useful purpose. As between the appropriators the one first in time has the right. A person who desires to appropriate water must post a notice at the point of the intended diversion, stating amount, purpose and means by which he intends to divert it, and must begin work on such ditch, pipe or acqueduct as he intends to use, and must continue such work until finished, unless temporarily interrupted by snow or rain. He must also file a copy of the notice above mentioned within ten days with the recorder of the county in which said notice is posted. A failure to comply with this rule deprives the claimant of the right as against a subsequent claimant who does.

U. S. Mining Laws.

OIL IS PLACER.—Placer claims may be made for petroleum, etc.

CHAP. 216.—An Act to authorize the entry and patenting of lands containing petroleum and other mineral oils under the placer mining laws of the United States.

That any person authorized to enter lands under the mining laws of the United States may enter and obtain patent to lands containing petroleum or other mineral oils, and chiefly valuable therefor, under the provisions of the laws relating to placer mineral claims; PROVIDED,

That lands containing such petroleum or other mineral oils which have heretofore been filed upon, claimed or improved as mineral, but not yet patented, may be held and patented under the provisions of this act the same as if such filing, claim or improvement were subsequent to the date of the passage thereof.

[Approved, February 11, 1897.]

ALIEN MINE OWNERS.—The following law in United States Territories is in force.

CHAP. 363.—An Act to better define and regulate the rights of aliens to hold and own real estate in the Territories.

That no alien or person who is not a citizen of the United States, or who has not declared his intention to become a citizen of the United States in the manner prescribed by law shall acquire title to or own any land in any Territory of the United States except as hereinafter provided. * * * * *

SEC. 2. That this Act shall not apply to land now owned in any of the Territories of the United States by aliens, which was acquired on or before March 3d, 1887, so long as it is held by the then owners, their heirs or legal representatives, nor to any alien who shall become a bona fide resident of the United States, and any alien who shall become a bona fide resident of the United States, or shall have declared his intention to become a citizen of the United States in the manner provided by law, shall have

73

the right to acquire and hold lands in either of the Territories of the United States upon the same terms as citizens of the United States; PROVIDED:

That if any such resident alien shall cease to be a bona fide resident of the United States then such alien shall have 10 years from the time he ceases to be such bona fide resident in which to alienate such lands.

This Act shall not be construed to prevent any persons not citizens of the United States from acquiring or holding lots or parcels of lands in any incorporated or platted city, town, or village, or in any mine or mining claim, in any of the Territories of the United States.

[Approved March 2, 1897.]

WHAT LOCATED.—§2319.—All valuable mineral deposits in lands belonging to the United States, both surveyed and unsur. veyed, are hereby declared to be free and open to exploration and purchase, and the lands in which they are found to occupation and purchase, by citizens of the United States and those who have declared their intention to become such, under regulations prescribed by law, and according to the

LOCAL RULES.—Local customs or rules of miners in the several mining districts, so far as the same are applicable and not inconsistent with the laws of the United States.—§1, May 10, 1872

QUARTZ.—§2320.—Mining claims upon veins or lodes of quartz or other rock in place bearing gold, silver, cinnabar, lead, tin, copper or other valuable deposits, heretofore located, shall be governed as to length along the vein or lode by the customs, regulations, and laws in force at the date of their location. A mining claim located after the tenth day of May, eighteen hundred and seventy-two whether located by one or more persons, may equal but not exceed, one thousand five hundred feet in length along the vein or lode.

MUST DISCOVER.—No location of a mining claim shall be made until the discovery of the vein or lode within the limits of the claim located. No claim shall extend more than three hundred feet on each side of the middle of the vein at the surface, nor shall any claim be limited by any mining regulation to less than twenty-five feet on each side of the middle of the vein at the surface, except where adverse rights existing on the tenth day of May, 1872, render such limitation necessary. The end lines of each claim shall be parallel to each other. –§2, May 10, 1872.

CITIZENSHIP.—§2321.—Proof of citizenship, under this chapter, may consist, in the case of an individual, of his own affidavit thereof; in the case of an association of persons unincorporated, of the affidavit of their authorized agent, made on his own knowledge, or upon information and belief; and in the case of a corporation organized under the laws of the United States, or of any State or Territory thereof, by the filing of a certified copy of their charter or certificate of incorporation.—§7, May 10, 1872.

APEX, SURFACE, DIP AND SIDE VEINS.—§2322.—The locators of all mining locations heretofore made or which shall hereafter be made, on any mineral vein, lode, or ledge, situated on the public domain, their heirs and assigns, where no adverse claim exists on the tenth day of May, 1872, so long as they comply with the laws of the United States, and with State, Territorial, and local regulations not in conflict with the laws of the United States governing their possessory title, shall have the exclusive right of possession and enjoyment of all the surface included within the lines of their locations, and of all veins, lodes, and ledges throughout their entire depth, the top or apex of which lies inside of such surface-lines extended downward vertically, although such veins, lodes or ledges may so far depart from a perpendicular in their course downward as to extend outside the vertical side lines of such surface locations. But their right of possession to such outside parts of such veins or ledges shall be confined to such portions thereof as lie between vertical planes drawn downward as above described, through the end lines of their locations, so continued in their own direction that such planes will intersect such exterior parts of such veins or ledges. And

75

nothing in this section shall authorize the locator or possessor of a vein or lode which extends in its downward course beyond the vertical lines of his claim to enter upon the surface of a claim owned or possessed by another.—¾3, May 10, 1872.

TUNNELS.—¾232.—Where a tunnel is run for the development of a vein or lode, or for the discovery of mines, the owners of such tunnel shall have the right of possession of all veins or lodes within 3,000 feet from the face of such tunnel on the line thereof, not previously known to exist, discovered in such tunnel, to the same extent as if discovered from the surface; and locations on the line of such tunnel of veins or lodes not appearing on the surface, made by other parties after the commencement of the tunnel, and while the same is being prosecuted with reasonable diligence, shall be invalid; but failure to prosecute the work on the tunnel, for six months shall be considered as an abandonment of the right to all undiscovered veins on the line of such tunnel.—¾4, May 10, 1872.

LOCATION, LABOR AND RULES.—¾2324.—The miners of each mining district may make regulations not in conflict with the laws of the United States, or with the State or Territory in which the district is situated, governing the location, manner of recording, amount of work necessary to hold possession of a mining-claim, subject to the following requirements: The location must be distinctly marked on the ground so that its boundaries can be readily traced.

RECORD.—records of mining claims hereafter made shall contain the name or names of the locators, the date of the location, and such a description of the claim or claims located by reference to some natural object or permanent monument as will identify the claim.

ANNUAL LABOR.—On each claim located after the tenth day of May, 1872, and until a patent has been issued therefor, not less than one hundred dollars' worth of labor shall be performed or improvements made during each year. On all claims located prior to the tenth day of May, 1872, ten dollars' worth of labor shall be performed or improvements made by the first day of January, 1875, and each year thereafter, for each 100 feet in length along the vein until a patent has been issued therefor, but where such claims are held in common, such expenditure may be made upon any one claim; and upon a failure to comply with these conditions, the claim or mine upon which such failure occurred shall be open to relocation in the same manner as if no location of the same had ever been made, provided that the original locators, their heirs, assigns, or legal representatives, have not resumed work upon the claim after failure and before such location. Upon the failure of any one of several co-owners to contribute his proportion of the expenditures required hereby, the co-owners who have performed the labor or made the improvements may, at the expiration of the year, give such delinquent co-owner personal notice in writing or notice by publication in the newspaper published nearest the claim, for at least once a week for ninety days, and if at the expiration of ninety days after such notice in writing or by publication such delinquent should fail or refuse to contribute his proportion of the expenditure required by this section, his interest in the claim shall become the property of his co-owners who have made the required expenditures.—§5, May 10, 1872.

LABOR BY TUNNEL.—A person or company may run a tunnel for the purposes of developing a lode or lodes, owned by said person or company, the money so expended in said tunnel shall be taken and considered as expended on said lode or lodes, whether located prior to or since the passage of said act; and such person or company shall not be required to perform work on the surface of said lode or lodes in order to hold the same as required by said act.—§1, February 11, 1875.

ANNUAL LABOR BEGINS.—"Provided, That the period within which the work required to be done annually on all unpatented mineral claims shall commence on the first day of January succeeding the date of location of such claim, and this section shall apply to all claims located since May 10, 1872."

APPLICATION FOR PATENT.—$2325.—A patent for any land claimed and located for valuable deposits may be obtained in the following manner: Any person, association, or corporation authorized to locate a claim under this chapter, having claimed and located a piece of land for such purposes, who has or have, complied with the terms of this chapter, may file in the proper land office an application for a patent, under oath, showing such compliance, together with a plat and field-notes of the claim or claims in common, made by or under the direction of the United States Surveyor-General, showing accurately the boundaries of the claim or claims which shall be distinctly marked by monuments on the ground, and shall post a copy of such plat, together with a notice of such application for a patent, in a conspicuous place on the land embraced in such plat previous to the filing of the application for a patent, and shall file an affidavit of at least two persons that such notice has been duly posted, and shall file a copy of the notice in such land-office, and shall thereupon be entitled to a patent for the land in the manner following:

60 DAYS' PUBLICATION.—The Register of the land office, upon the filing of such application, plat, field-notes, notices, and affidavits, shall publish a notice that such application has been made for the period of sixty days, in a newspaper to be by him designated as published nearest to such claim; and he shall also post such notice in his office for the same period. The claimant at the time of filing this application, or at any time thereafter, within the sixty days of publication, shall file with the Register a certificate of the United States Surveyor-General

$500 IMPROVEMENTS.—That $500 worth of labor has been expended or improvements made upon the claim by himself or grantors; that the plat is correct, with such further description by such reference to natural objects or permanent monuments as shall identify the claim, and furnish an accurate description, to be incorporated in the patent. At the expiration of the sixty days of publication the claimant shall file his affidavit, showing that the plat and notice have been posted in a conspicuous place on the claim during such period of publication.

ADVERSE CLAIM.—If no adverse claim shall have been filed with the Register and the Receiver of the proper land-office at the expiration of the sixty days of publication, it shall be assumed that the applicant is entitled to a patent, upon the payment to the proper officer of

$5 PER ACRE.—Five dollars per acre, and that no adverse claim exists; and thereafter no objection from third parties to the issuance of a patent shall be heard, except it be shown that the applicant has failed to comply with the terms of this chapter.—¿6, May 10, 1872.

¿2325 AMENDED.—"Provided, That where the claimant for a patent is not a resident of or within the land district wherein the vein, lode, ledge or deposit sought to be patented is located, the application for patent and the affidavits required to be made in this section by the

NON-RESIDENT.—Claimant for such patent may be made by his, her or its authorized agent, where said agent is conversant with the facts sought to be established by said affidavits: And provided, That this section shall apply to all applications now pending for patents to mineral lands."—¿1, January 22, 1880.

ADVERSE CLAIMS.—¿2326.—Where an adverse claim is filed during the period of publication, it shall be upon oath of the person or persons making the same, and shall show the nature, boundaries, and extent of such adverse claim, and all proceedings, except the publication of notice and making and filing of the affidavit thereof, shall be stayed until the controversy shall have been settled or decided by a court of competent jurisdiction, or the adverse claim waived.

SUIT IN 30 DAYS.—It shall be the duty of the adverse claimant, within thirty days after filing his claim, to commence proceedings in a court of competent jurisdiction, to determine the question of the right of possession, and prosecute the same with reasonable diligence to final judgment; and a failure so to do shall be a waiver of his adverse claim.

AFTER JUDGMENT.—After such judgment shall have been rendered, the party entitled to the possession of the claim, or any portion thereof, may, without giving further notice, file a certified copy of the judgment-roll with the Register of the land-office, together with the certificate of the Surveyor-General that the requisite amount of labor has been expended or improvements made thereon, and the description required in other cases, and shall pay to the Receiver

$5 PER ACRE.—$5 per acre for his claim, together with the proper fees, whereupon the whole proceedings and the judgment-roll shall be certified by the Register to the Commissioner of the General Land-Office, and a patent shall issue thereon for the claim, or such portion thereof as the applicant shall appear, from the decision of the court, to rightly possess. If it appears from the decision of the court that several parties are entitled to separate and different portions of the claim, each party may pay for his portion of the claim, with the proper fees, and file the certificate and description by the Surveyor-General, whereupon the Register shall certify the proceedings and judgment-roll to the Commissioner of the General Land Office, as in the preceding case, and patents shall issue to the several parties according to their respective rights. Nothing herein contained shall be construed to prevent the alienation of the title conveyed by a patent for a mining claim to any person whatever.—§7. May 10, 1872.

§2326 AMENDED.—That if title to the ground in controversy shall not be established by either party, the jury shall so find, and judgment shall be entered according to the verdict. In such case cost shall not be allowed to either party, and the claimant shall not proceed in the land-office or be entitled to a patent for the ground in controversy until he shall have perfected his title. —March 3, 1881.

§2326 AMENDED.—The oath of any duly-authorized agent or attorney-in-fact of the adverse claimant cognizant of the facts stated; and the adverse claimant, if residing or at the time being beyond the limits of the district wherein the claim is situated, may make oath to the adverse claim before the clerk of any court of record of the United States or of the State or Territory where the adverse claimant may then be, or before any notary public of such State or Territory.—§1, April 26, 1882.

IDEM.—AFFIDAVITS OUT OF LAND DISTRICT.—That applicants for mineral patents, if residing beyond the limits of the district wherein the claim is situated, may make any oath or affidavit required for proof of citizenship before the clerk of any court of record or before any notary public of any State or Territory.—§2 Id.

SURVEY.—§2327.—The description of vein or lode claims, upon surveyed lands, shall designate the location of the claim with reference to the lines of the public surveys, but need not conform therewith; but where a patent shall be issued for claims upon unsurveyed lands, the Surveyor-General, in extending the surveys, shall adjust the same to the boundaries of such patented claim, according to the plat or description thereof, but so as in no case to interfere with or change the location of any such patented claim.—§8, May 10, 1872.

PLACERS OPEN TO ENTRY.—§2329.—Claims usually called "placers," including all forms of deposit, excepting veins of quartz, or other rock in place, shall be subject to entry and patent, under like circumstances and conditions, and upon similar proceedings, as are provided for vein or lode claims; but where the lands have been previously surveyed by the United States, the entry in its exterior limits shall conform to the legal subdivisions of public lands.—§12, July 9, 1870.

SUBDIVISION.—§2330.—Legal subdivisions of forty acres may be subdivided into ten-acre tracts; and two or more persons, or associations of persons, having contiguous claims of any size, although such claims may be less than ten acres each, may make joint entry thereof; but

160 ACRE PLACERS.—No location of a placer claim, made after July, 9, 1870, shall exceed 160 acres for any one person or associa-

tion of persons, which location shall conform to the United
States surveys; and nothing in this section contained shall
defeat or impair any bona fide pre-emption or homestead claim
upon agricultural lands, or authorize the sale of the improvements of any bona fide settler to any purchaser.—§12, July 9, 1870.

SURVEYED LANDS.—§2331.—Where placer claims are upon surveyed lands, and conform to legal subdivisions, no further survey or plat shall be required, and all placer mining claims
located after May 10, 1872, shall conform as near as practicable
with the United States system of public land surveys, and the
rectangular subdivisions of such surveys, and no such location
shall include more than twenty acres for each individual
claimant; but where placer claims cannot be conformed to legal
subdivisions, survey and plat shall be made as on unsurveyed
lands and where by the segregation

FARM AND MINERAL.—Of mineral land in any legal subdivision
a quantity of agricultural land less than forty acres remains,
such fractional portion of agricultural land may be entered by
any party qualified by law, for homestead or pre-emption
purposes. §10, May 10, 1872.

PLACER WITH LODE.—§2333—Where the same person, association, or corporation is in possession of a placer claim, and also a
vein or lode included within the boundaries thereof, application
shall be made for a patent for the placer claim, with the statement that it includes such vein or lode, and in such case a patent
shall issue for the placer claim, subject to the provisions of this
chapter, including such vein or lode, upon the payment of five
dollars per acre for such vein or lode claim, and twenty-five feet
of surface on each side thereof. The remainder of the placer
claim, or any placer claim not embracing any

PLACERS $2.50 PER ACRE.—Vein or lode claim, shall be paid for
at the rate of $2.50 per acre, together with all costs of proceedings;
and where a vein or lode, such as described in §2320, is known to
exist within the boundaries of a placer claim, an application for
a patent for such placer claim which does not include an

application for the vein or lode claim shall be construed as a conclusive declaration that the claimant of the placer claim has no right of possession of the vein or lode claim; but where the existence of a vein or lode in a placer claim is not known, a patent for the placer claim shall convey all valuable mineral and other deposits within the boundaries thereof.—§11, May 10, 1872.

DEPUTY SURVEYOR. §2334. The Surveyor-General of the United States may appoint in each land district containing mineral lands as many competent surveyors as shall apply for appointment to survey mining claims. The expenses of the survey of vein or lode claims, and the survey and subdivision of placer claims into smaller quantities than 160 acres, together with the cost of publication of notices, shall be paid by the applicants, and they shall be at liberty to obtain the same at the most reasonable rates, and they shall also be at liberty to employ any United States deputy surveyor to make the survey. The Commissioner of the General Land-Office

CHARGES.—Shall also have power to establish the maximum charges for surveys and publication of notices under this chapter; and, in case of excessive charges for publication, he may designate any newspaper published in a land district where mines are situated for the publication of mining notices in such district, and fix the rates to be charged by such paper; and, to the end that the Commissioner may be fully informed on the subject, each applicant shall file with the Register a sworn statement of all charges and fees paid by such applicant for surveys, together with all fees and money paid the Register and the Receiver of the Land-Office, which statement shall be transmitted, with the other papers in the case, to the Commissioner of the General Land-Office.—§12, May 10, 1872.

PROOFS.—§2335.—All affidavits required to be made under this chapter may be verified before any officer authorized to administer oaths within the land district where the claims may be situated, and all testimony and proofs may be taken before any such officer, and, when duly certified by the officer taking the same, shall have the same force and effect as if taken before the Register and Receiver of the land office. In cases of contest as to the mineral or agricultural character of land,

AGRICULTURAL CONTEST.—The testimony and proofs may be taken as herein provided on personal notice of at least ten days to the opposing party; or if such party cannot be found, then by publication of at least once a week for thirty days in a newspaper, to be designated by the Register of the Land Office as published nearest to the location of such land; and the Register shall require proof that such notice has been given.—§13, May 10, 1872.

CROSS VEINS.—§2336.—Where two or more veins intersect or cross each other, priority of title shall govern, and such prior location shall be entitled to all ore or mineral contained within the space of intersection; but the subsequent location shall have the right of way through the space of intersection for the purposes of the convenient working of the mine. And

VEINS UNITING.—Where two or more veins unite, the oldest or prior location shall take the vein below the point of union, including all the space of intersection.—§14, May 10, 1872.

MILL-SITES.—§2337.—Where non-mineral land not contiguous to the vein or lode is used or occupied by the proprietor of such vein or lode for mining or milling purposes, such non-adjacent surface ground may be embraced and included in an application for a patent for such vein or lode, and the same may be patented therewith, subject to the same preliminary requirements as to survey and notice as are applicable to veins or lodes; but no location hereafter made of such non-adjacent land shall exceed five acres, and payment for the same must be made at the same rate as fixed by this chapter for the superficies of the lode. The owner of a quartz mill or reduction works, not owning a mine in connection therewith, may also receive a patent for his mill-site, as provided in this section.—§15, May 10, 1872.

STATES EXCEPTED—§2345—Michigan, Wisconsin, Missouri, Kansas, Alabama and Minnesota.

84